Ancient Rituals of Nature Religion

Here is a charming collection of magical practices and rituals, invented or adapted by the author. Its style is poetic, and deliberately archaic—that is, designed to sound as if it might have have been written in an earlier century—as seems appropriate to the works of a "Crone" or old Wise Woman.

This book appeals to the imagination, as well as gives practical directions for the application or performance of numerous spells, charms, recipes, or rituals. Generally these are based on familiar ideas and materials, and easy to carry out. They do not depend on any particular belief or system, but take their inspiration from nature and folklore.

No special knowledge or training is necessary for the practitioner, and the book may also be read simply for pleasure, contemplation, or spiritual refreshment.

This book relates powerful ancient practices, especially those of the old Nature Religions, to a modern appreciation of the world around us. It might even be seen as a kind of magical ecology, in which every manifestation of nature may be valued spiritually as well as cherished for its role in the environment. In a world where nature is so often slighted or ignored, this book serves to heighten the reader's awareness of the magic lying beneath the surface, and the powerful ties that exist between mind and matter, even in modern times.

This quaint and charming book is appealing to anyone attracted to ancient lore and occult rituals, and its value lies in the fact that it is not limited to any specific beliefs or practices.

Accessible to a wide variety of readers, as it depends largely on the materials of nature and their ability to reflect and enhance human states of mind, *The Crone's Book of Wisdom* is more than a "how-to" manual. The poetic and imaginative style makes it a powerful reading experience as well.

About Valerie Worth

The author is primarily a poet, with a strong belief in the power of the imagination to enrich life in all its aspects. She has studied the natural world in some depth, and found marked correspondences between its phenomena and the workings of the human mind and spirit. She has lived in a variety of places, including India, and drawn upon the ideas and philosophies of many cultures.

To Write to the Author

We cannot guarantee that every letter written to the author can be answered, but all will be forwarded. Both the author and the publisher appreciate hearing from readers, learning of your enjoyment and benefit from this book. Llewellyn also publishes a bi-monthly news magazine with news and reviews of practical esoteric studies and articles helpful to the student, and some readers' questions and comments to the author may be answered through this magazine's columns if permission to do is included in the original letter. The author sometimes participates in seminars and workshops, and dates and places are announced in *The Llewellyn New Times*. To write to the author, or to ask a question, write to:

Valerie Worth
c/o THE LLEWELLYN NEW TIMES
P.O. Box 64383-892, St. Paul, MN 55164-0383, U.S.A.

Please enclose a self-addressed, stamped envelope for reply, or $1.00 to cover costs.

About Llewellyn's Practical Magick Series

To some people, the idea that "Magick" is *practical* comes as a suprise.

It shouldn't. The entire basis for Magick is to exercise influence over one's environment. While Magick is also, and properly so, concerned with spiritual growth and psychological transformation, even the spiritual life must rest firmly on material foundations.

The material world and the psychic are intertwined, and it is this very fact that establishes the Magickal Link: that the psychic can as easily influence the material as vice versa.

Magick can, and should, be used in one's daily life for better living! Each of us has been given Mind and Body, and surely we are under Spiritual obligation to make full usage of these wonderful gifts. Mind and Body work together, and Magick is simply the extension of this interaction into dimensions beyond the limits normally conceived. That's why we commonly talk of the "supernormal" in connection with domain of Magick.

The Body is alive, and all Life is an expression of the Divine. There is God-power in the Body and in the Earth, just as there is in Mind and Spirit. With Love and Will, we use Mind to link these aspects of Divinity together to bring about change.

With Magick we increase the flow of Divinity in our lives and in the world around us. We add to the beauty of it all—for to work Magick we must work in harmony with the Laws of Nature and of the Psyche. *Magick is the flowering of the Human Potential.*

Practical Magick is concerned with the Craft of Living well and in harmony with Nature, and with the Magick of the Earth, in the things of the Earth, in the seasons and cycles and in the things we make with hand and Mind.

Other Books by Valerie Worth

The Crone's Book of Words, 1971 (Llewellyn)

Llewellyn's Practical Magick Series

THE CRONE'S BOOK OF WISDOM

Valerie Worth

1988
Llewellyn Publications
St. Paul, Minnesota, 55164-0383, U.S.A.

International Standard Book Number: 0-87542-892-4
Library of Congress Catalog Number: 88-45194

First Edition, 1988
First Printing, 1988

Library of Congress Cataloging-in-Publication Data

Worth, Valerie.
    The Crone's book of wisdom.

    (Llewellyn's practical magick series)
      1. Herbs—Folklore. 2. Charms. 3. Incantations.
I. Title. II. Series.
GR780.W68   1988   398'.353   88-45194
ISBN 0-87542-892-4

Cover Design: Terry Buske

Produced by Llewellyn Publications
Typography and Art property of Chester-Kent, Inc.

Published by
LLEWELLYN PUBLICATIONS
A Division of Chester-Kent, Inc.
P.O. Box 64383
St. Paul, MN 55164-0383, U.S.A.

Printed in the United States of America

Contents

Introduction

Of the Pleasures and
Virtues in these Works

This book contains much matter concerning what may well be done, from day to day, in the practice of the magical arts, not only such high activity of spirit as shall inspire and enlighten, but also certain ways in which the hands may work to create from earthly substance a fair array of objects and inventions, both immediately useful and potentially of vast power. There is pleasure in the fashioning of these things, and pleasure also in their further employment. Sprung in simple form from the hands, they return great nourishment to the spirit, being both well made and well conceived.

Such entities as herb brews, potions, oils, charms, candles, amulets, robes, etc., shall act well in themselves to please and serve. Yet also, when they are incorporated into larger acts of the imagination, as in certain arcane ceremonies ultimately to be described, it shall be seen that all the spirit's wisdom may be made manifest by the artful use of these materials.

Thus the virtues of Great Wisdom may enlighten the hands as readily as the spirit, and when hands and spirit are instructed and prepared they may act as one to raise from humble works a larger realm of magic—minor artifacts transformed into symbols of universal meaning, based ever upon the homeliest of recipes—whereby an herb may grow to touch the very Sun, or a single candle light the dead back into the living cosmos.

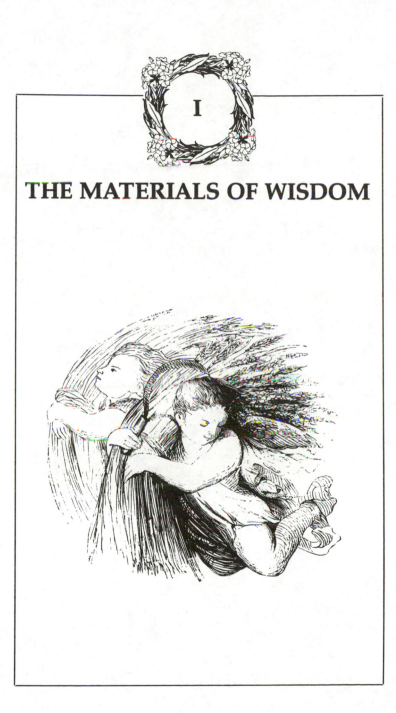

I

THE MATERIALS OF WISDOM

Here Shall Be told the method and the substance, the means and requirements, for certain arts of benefit to both the body and the mind, used ordinarily and daily, yet also in rites and observations of an elevated nature. If these instructions are attended and remembered, the practices envisioned further in this book shall be assumed with greater ease and clarity.

Herb Brews

It is better that the herbs from our gardens or the wild woods and fields be taken in this way—drunk fresh in all their strength—than wasted and weakened in flavorings for victuals, thus to comfort only the vain palate. These brews are true powers, whereas the same herbs cooked in food are poor wraiths of themselves. Honor them as they deserve, and they shall not fail.

The fair leaves or other necessary parts should be gathered as young and fair as possible, and a handful placed in a plain brown teapot of good size. Fill the pot then with fresh-boiling water, and allow this tea to steep for twelve minutes by the hourglass or clock. Pour it out then straightaway into a cup; sweeten it with a teaspoonful of honey, and drink the infusion while it is hot.

A few of the well-known herbs that may be used for such purposes follow here:

Anise, the Amorous: The seeds, to strengthen passions

Basil, the Courageous: Against faintness of heart

Borage, the Inspiring: Against aches in the limbs

Caraway, the Sweet: The seeds, for mental vigor

Catnip, the Subtle: Against fever and chills

Mint, the Comforting: Against afflictions of the stomach

Nasturtium, the Pungent: Against the headache

Parsley, the Stout: Against pallor and frailty

Red Clover, the Succulent: The flowers, for good temper

Rosemary, the Fair: To soothe the nerves

Rue, the Mysterious: To assuage guilt and sorrow

Sage, the Powerful: Against melancholy and distress of the mind

Thyme, the Sovereign: Against coughs

White Pine, the Healthful: Against colds and catarrh

Wild Ginger, the Profound: The root, against lassitude

An Elixir of Honey

To strengthen the constitution and dispel afflictions of the mind and body, this honey elixir has no equal. It is pure and wholesome, and may be taken as a tonic by children, grown men and women, and ancients alike, with good results. Concoct it thus:

Boil in eight ounces of water the fresh leaves of sage, thyme, and mint, a large spoonful of each, until of liquid there be left but an ounce or two. Pour off this brew, and when it is cool add to it a teaspoonful of good brown cider vinegar, and also three ounces of honey, strained fresh from the comb. Stir these well until the honey is blended and the whole shines clear. Then it may be sipped, from a wine glass, all or in part. If any is not used, it may be kept in a tightly corked vessel for later draughts.

SAGE

On Using Wild Herbs for Practical
and Magical Purposes

Certain plants of the commonest sort may be of great use in the procuring of both physical and spiritual benefits. It would be superfluous to treat at length here those cultivated herbs all gardeners know, powerful though they be for tonics and teas; yet those other plants, the lowly stalks many ignore by the path or roadside, or from which they idly strip the leaves with no thought of what treasures they cast down, may serve the Wise most faithfully.

Cherish then those leaves, flowers, or other parts that are healthful, and pluck them at their height, to be dried and brewed as teas, or otherwise used as will be directed. Those that are of value in their spiritual aspects may be prepared and duly fashioned into charms, and kept carefully, as will be described.

Here follow some whose virtues are undeniable, yet too little honored by most persons (who surely ever have need of them).

The yellow **Avens**, called also **Geum**, has a modest flower which yet produces pertinacious hooked seeds. Take then its manner as a pattern, and bind twenty-two of these seeds in a small bag of gauze, to call forth strength of purpose from even the most malleable of natures.

The leaves of the **Bayberry** will produce a vigorous tea, of healthful flavor and inspiriting vapor, good to be taken by those who require renewal in the midst of misfortune. The silver frosted berries may be boiled a while in rainwater and the freed wax then skimmed off the surface. This wax mixed with a pure oil will make a balm of value for soothing the skin, and hence the mind.

Bedstraw, its stalks starred along their length by radiating leaves, should be laid beneath the pillow, secretly, to strengthen a failing marriage.

The **Bindweed**, unwrapped from some other plant to which it clings, may be thrice knotted and thus kept to assure the fidelity of a lover. If it should break at all in the knotting, it must be cast away and another strand of the weed gathered. Yet if three strands should thus break, it shall be a sign that this lover is weak and unworthy of your attentions.

The **Black Mustard**, a plant of great vigor, may be dried and worn in a bag about the neck for safety from illness and misadventure. It shall also be of value when held in the hand during an eclipse of the Sun, assuring that no evil influence may enter into one upon whom the Moon's shadow falls.

Burrs of the **Burdock**, packed in a wooden box, must inspire honesty in one to whom they are given. There is also another use that shall be shown later in this book.

The **Buttercup**, its blossoms filled to overflowing with the Sun's benisons, shall confer a harmony as of milk and honey upon the household where a bunch is hung over the doorway, and the falling petals allowed to remain for a week upon the threshold.

Use the golden sap of the **Celandine** as a powerful ink, especially for charmed inscriptions upon parchment or fine leather.

The lowly **Chickweed**, flowering like small stars tangled in the meadow grasses, may yield a tea of noble nourishment; also let it be wound into a garland and hung about the neck to attract the favors of the Heavens.

Cut ten strong stalks of blue-flowered **Chicory** with a sharp knife and bind them about from top to bottom with a cord. This wand should then be given to one who is ill that he may be strengthened in blood, flesh, and bone.

All **Cinquefoils** assist the works of magic. Sprigs thick-leaved should be held in the hand for some moments before the inception of any spiritual task, and likewise after such an undertaking is completed.

The **Daisy** is named Flower of the White Sun, and all endeavors of high virtue may be better accomplished by its influence. Where this plant blooms, you shall walk about it thrice and name it as it is named here. Take away a single flower, from which the petals should then be plucked and pressed in a white paper. Thereafter swallow one petal each day, again naming the name, until all shall be consumed and your own pure fire thereby strengthened.

Collect some white sap from stalks of the **Dandelion**, and mix it with a little cow's milk as a bitter potion—this to be performed and taken when you would chasten greed and pride, lest these faults lead you from the ways of truth.

The **Fringed Loosestrife** shall yield inner peace to one who gathers it from the roadside and wears it on the breast for seven days.

Goatsbeard, combining powers of the Sun and Moon, as its head is first gold-rayed and then silver-globed, should be plucked in both guises and the stems' juices pressed upon your palms. Thus shall the right hand and the left hand both serve you well.

Ground Ivy, called also *Gill-over-the-Ground*, may be brewed into a bitter tea and sipped, to overcome weakness and timidity. Strewn about the floors of the house, these leaves will promote serenity and benign dreams.

The **Heal-All**, also called *Self-Heal*, is in all its parts most fervent as a favorable charm. Dried, tied up in a bag of purple silk and hung on a cord about the neck, it will soothe the stomach, clear the consciousness, enliven the eye, and guard the hand from hesitation. Treat this good herb with esteem and it shall not fail.

The **Jewelweed**, also called *Touch-Me-Not*, and also *Orange Balsam*, provides a most excellent lotion for afflictions of the skin, particularly ivy poisoning. Crush the whole plant and press its juices upon the malady, then bind on a good number of the leaves, bruised, as a poultice. This should be left in place from dawn to dawn.

Beware the powerful **Jimsonweed**, an ancient poison. Shun its touch, yet wearing a glove uproot it and carry it to the rat's tunnel. Forthwith thrust it in, and drive it deep below with an iron rod or stake. This should then be repeated with further stalks until the space is filled, which will thus be of great efficacy in driving away the thieving vermin.

Take berried branches of the **Juniper** at the Winter Solstice and hang them over your doorway for thirteen days. Then take them down and pluck the berries therefrom, saving these in a small box, in honor of life renewed. Keep them well all the year, until the Winter Solstice comes again, when they should be solemnly burned and the same gathering of branches performed anew.

The elegant **Lady's Thumb**, as it grows perfect and chaste in the worst of waste places, shall be plucked and kept for a charm against all foulness and corruption.

Lady's Sorrel, called also *Sourgrass*, may well be eaten as it grows, for health and a clear intelligence, or else be brewed into a broth, with a little salt added, to the same end.

The **May Apple**, called also *False Mandrake*, may be used for the same purposes of sorcery as the true and deadly Mandrake or Mandragora. While its fruit is benign, it serves also magically, whereby it should be dried and pierced with spines of the Hawthorn as an object of spite. The root is a source of poison, and may be employed in a dire charm later prescribed within this book.

The fragrant **Melilot**, called also *Sweet Clover*, both white and yellow varieties, should be gathered in great bunches when it flowers, and hung upon the walls of every chamber in your house. Thus will its scent prove a benison to you for many months thereafter.

When the **Milkweed** buds and blooms along the dusty roadside, its emanations are as of the costliest perfume; yet who, passing by, shall think to savor it? Gather then an immense bouquet, and set it soon in water within your house. This attention shall be rewarded by such sweetening of the air that all evil shall be driven from your spirit, and you shall be thus blessed as long as the fragrance shall last.

The clever **Mistletoe**, of berries white and leaves substantial, shall render powerless your staunchest enemy if you will keep it hung above your bed; and later in this book a further charm shall yet be told.

A stiff sprig of **Motherwort**, rough with leaves, ripe-seeded and sharp husked, should be carried to the place where a woman lies in labor. Its keen barbs are scratched lightly upon each of her palms; two leaves are laid upon her brow, and a leaf given her in either hand to grasp. Thus shall she be succoured by the Earth, who stands Midwife of midwives to all life.

Pound well in a mortar the fresh leaves of **Mullein**, and make of them a poultice for infections, warts, and rashes of the skin. These wooly leaves, whole, may be used in charms attracting fertility and prosperity to those whose lands grow dry and barren.

A few seeds of **Peppergrass** should be chewed to cure the headache. They may also be used as a charm for wealth.

Pluck up the lowly **Pineapple Weed** by its poor roots, and crush it in the hands; such fruitful fragrance shall thereby be liberated as shall renew forgotten hope and expectation, and inspire the hands to strengthened works.

The **Plantain** of common growth, its hardy spike

arising from broad leaves, shall, when decocted to a lotion with rain water, and rubbed upon the skin, invigorate the whole flesh to a condition of redemption, and the senses to a state of exhaltation.

Gather the spiked leaves of **Prickly Lettuce** and dry them well, then crush them, and they may be burned as an incense to renew the senses and heal the wounded spirit.

Brew the young leaves of **Queen Anne's Lace** (taking care that it be indeed this herb itself, and not one of those, as the notorious Hemlock, which resembles it but yields an extreme poison) and thus produce a tea of very healthful flavor and properties. The petals of the dried blossoms, scattered throughout the house, shall work a beneficial influence on all who live therein.

Those who suffer in summer from the pollen of the **Ragweed** should take the plant before it flowers, break it small, and pound these fragments to a dust. A pinch of this powder placed, on each of seven mornings, upon the left palm, while the word LAEDO is uttered, shall serve to weaken the plant's powers over the afflicted.

St. Johnswort, an herb of ancient repute, may simply be carried in the pocket as a powerful charm against all evil. Otherwise it is useful as a beneficial bath, if the leaves and flowers are infused in a tubful of water and the whole body immersed therein.

The **Sandbur**, called also *Sand Spur*, whose hurtful spines will sting the careless foot, may yet bring an assuagement of pain to the grieving and heartsore.

Wrap three of these burrs in a lock of Lamb's Wool and keep these in a small bag of leather hung about the neck, for the length of three lunar months. So shall the viper sorrow be vanquished.

Scrub the teeth with a split twig of **Sassafras** for cleanliness of the mouth and facility of speech. Flatten three of its lobed leaves within a book, and later hang them in your window against the works of evil wizards; boil its twigs in water to produce a lotion of benefit to the skin. In all ways this plant shall be of service to you and further your well-being.

The **Stinging Nettle**, which must in wisdom be avoided for its malevolent properties, yet shall yield a nutritious tea if the leaves are plucked young (by hands safeguarded in gloves the while). Also it may work a fitting revenge upon one who has betrayed you, if a box full of the stems, these wrapped in gaudy paper, be sent to the offender secretly at the waxing of the Moon.

The **Sunflower**, whether growing wild or boldly planted in the garden, may bestow great strength upon all who attend it. Let one plant be observed from day to day, and when its fire shall cool, its growth cease, and its seed be firm, cut the bowed head off with a hand's length of stalk remaining. Tie this tightly with a cord, and thus suspend it from a hook fixed to a ceiling within your house, that it may hang there all the winter and be well preserved. In the spring take it down, remove the seeds, and plant all but one of these in a great circle surrounding your house. The remaining seed you should then crack open and swallow the kernel thereof, thus to become one with its Sun-engendered flesh, while you live thereafter encircled by the new flowers that grow—yourself the fertile center of their solar influence.

The purple blooming **Thistle**, of many forms and sizes, is, like the Stinging Nettle, both vicious and mild. For its best use, take from it the sword-guarded flowers, when in the autumn they shall pale and open to silver silk. Collect this fine floss, and pack it into a small box, to be kept in readiness thereafter to treat any bleeding wound. Lay it soon, in abundance, upon the place, saying:

> Thistledown across thee
> Now comfort, stanch, and close thee.

The **Violet**, herb of beauty and true love, yields a tea of exquisite azure if the flowers be duly steeped in boiling water. This identical infusion is also to be used in preparing a ceremonial potion which will later in this book be described. Presently the recipe will be given for a charmed confection made from Violet blossoms.

Behold the motley **Viper's Bugloss**, of spired flowers fair to view yet frail, of spiny stems and leaves all pricking and bristling. One blossom from each of seven stalks, to be plucked and pressed dry within a sacred book, then kept in a folded paper over the heart, shall strengthen the immortal spirit.

The **Wild Rose** embodies such immutable sweetness and immaculate virtue that a tea made from its petals and given to any malefactor must change his very nature. Likewise a dust of rose-petals well-dried, pulverized, and mixed with a little powdered Orris-root, may be sprinkled in the bed of a contrary lover; so shall it turn love's vagaries to a faithful path again.

The **Woody Nightshade**, also called Bittersweet, has not the deadly character of the greater nightshades. Yet take it not for brew or potion, lest its kinship with these others work you harm. Use it, rather, for the comely and passionate appearance of its flowers and berries, as a charmed bouquet, to bestow where you would receive in return the amorous desires of a lover.

Leaves of the melancholy scented bone-pale **Yarrow** may serve as an aromatic to revive the fainting senses, or as a tea to slake the thirst of a fevered brain, but best of all as a reminder of mortality. Dried and hung up above the mirror where you most often see your face, it shall remain a chastisement to all ambitious vanities. Yet as Moon without Sun loses her strength, so yarrow's truth is incomplete. For the whole of wisdom, you must match it with the solar **Goldenrod**, gathering both at their height. Set them to dry within an earthen jar, to bloom and shine all winter, and favor you with signs of everlasting life. Thereby shall you be made all-wise, seeing that death, while potent, is not omnipotent.

The Creation of Charms

While the foregoing recipes for simple charms have taken sundry herbs as their basis, nearly any object may be used for such purposes if it be fitting in significance, duly prepared, and properly kept. Whether it be an herb, a pebble, a bone, a curl of dust, a pinch of Earth, a gem, an inscribed paper, or anything chosen cleverly to serve the desired intention, its power will lie as much in the inspiring properties which the object itself possesses, as in its ritual dedication. Thus while certain ancient and traditional charms may always be recommended, as particularly suited to certain needs, yet new ones may still be invented if the correspondence between object and necessity is imaginatively appropriate.

For a charm of high power and complexity it is best that a ritual incantation first be spoken over the object (or compatible combination of several objects) to release and direct its powers toward the realm in which they shall operate; then it may be anointed, or combined with some oil or balm of suitable scent, in a place of silence and secrecy, embellished by the presence of burning candles or an incense. Finally, the object (or objects) may be sewn up in a bag of cloth, or a small leather pouch, to be carried on the person, or worn about the neck, or hidden somewhere in safety; it may also be well guarded in a small wooden box upon which some further inscription has been set.

Any words originally spoken for the charm's dedication may be inscribed upon it, or repeated daily over it, thus strengthening its influence and the intention of its bearer. It should never be lost or forgotten, lest such neglect turn its powers awry; but if it be no longer needed, it should be carefully burned or buried with some fitting words of dismissal.

A later portion of this book will describe a number of highly elaborate and efficacious charms, their ingredients, mode of preparation, appropriate incantations, and all influences and circumstances under which they should be created.

The Creation of Talismans

The talismans envisioned in this book work much in the manner of charms, save that they bear certain specific inscriptions in which their power principally lies, the objects themselves being of less obvious significance. Thus a common pebble or small stone, of texture and form allowing the surface to be sufficiently inscribed, serves as well as any thing, and is easily discovered in the garden or even by the roadside.

Such a stone should be well scrubbed with soap and water, and dried completely. It may be covered with a white paint or left to its natural surface, upon which the inscription is set, either incised with a sharp instrument, or applied with colored paints if there be a symbolic design or picture, or with India ink where words are used. Generally both design and words together will serve with the best effect. The stone may be chosen for the value of its natural configuration, such as one of heart shape for a talisman pertaining to love, a crescent for some lunar influence, circular for the Sun, etc. When the talisman is completed, it should be ritually dedicated and preserved in the same fashion as a charm.

Further in this book will be found a collection of inscriptions, both verbal and pictorial, appropriate to such talismans.

Amulets and Magical Rings

An inscribed amulet is best worn about the neck (although some few are suited to the wrist or ankle) attached to a woven cord, a chain, or a leather thong. Thus a small medal or pendant, cut from some firm metal as copper or silver, will serve admirably. It will be ornamental, and is often worn openly, rather than hidden as would be a talisman or charm. However, any words in its inscription should be placed on the reverse side, worn next to the body, and only some symbolic design or image displayed upon the outward face. Thus a certain degree of secrecy will still be preserved; and when these words are written in the ancient Latin tongue, an even stronger obscurity will guard their purpose and protect their powers from dissipation.

An amulet of this nature is often used to celebrate some truth, or to affirm some belief, or to express some aspiration; it is seldom appropriate to the darker purposes—active revenge or malefaction (for these, a charm is always best suited). For example, to honor the Sun, to deny the power of death, to seek wisdom, to win love; all such are suited to the fair nature of these magical adornments.

In the matter of rings as well, any words should be inscribed on the inner surface thereof, with images upon the outward and visible side. A simple ring cut from a strip of metal, smoothed and shaped to a circle, is excellent for this purpose, and since it is worn openly, may also be given a highly decorative appearance.

Amulets and rings of metal may be engraved, or

they may be inscribed with paints and India ink in the same way as stone talismans. In this case, a protective lacquer should be applied over all to keep the inscription from wearing away.

When they are well fashioned and adapted to the nature of the ritual, these amulets and rings are worn to great advantage upon ceremonial occasions. Before such use, and even for less formal purposes, they may be dedicated and anointed in the same way as charms and talismans.

A number of appropriate inscriptions for amulets and rings will be given later in this book.

Scented Oils

All perfumes are of profound importance in directing the senses and the imagination toward specific ends. Every scent possesses its own character, and should not be used carelessly. Rather, it should be chosen scrupulously for its effect upon the occasion and the wearer. Cleverly used, a perfume will provide a powerful influence upon the circumstances surrounding its application, whether to a person or an object.

To prepare a pure and delicate scent, take some clear, light, odorless oil—one ounce—and warm it over the fire for six minutes, along with a large spoonful of aromatic woods, or roots, fragrant leaves or flowers (all first well dried, then crushed or pounded in a mortar). Let this mixture cool, then pour it out, to steep within a jar well sealed for twelve days thereafter. On the thirteenth day, strain it through fine cloth into a small basin; thence funnel it into a vial and stop this tight. If this preparation should not yield a strong enough perfume, as some occasions demand greater sharpness or pungency, certain essences of a less subtle nature may be bought and added to the original infusion—yet take care that such combinations be compatible, lest the pure character of the scent be sacrificed.

Such an oil may serve for anointments of the skin, either for ceremony, or for improved health, or simply for adornment. It may anoint candles to give them fragrance, or charms and other magical objects to consecrate them. It may be used also mixed into tinctures and balms, or with liquid wax when a new candle is being molded.

Each of the ceremonies presented later in this book requires the use of a specific scent in some form for its symbolic embellishment. When such a ritual is actually practiced, the efficacy of these perfumes becomes most evident.

Fragrant Tinctures

Take near three ounces of a strong, unscented alcohol and add to it whatever fragrant matter is chosen, whether leaves, roots, or flowers, thoroughly dried and crushed, or else some previously prepared scented oil, ten or twelve drops (or more, if the oil be faint). Shake these together well, and let stand twelve days, after which the tincture may be strained clear through a cloth.

Used for refreshment of the face and body, particularly before any ceremony, such a tincture will inspire the thoughts to strength, and the occasion to good issue.

The Preparation of Balms

Melt together, over a low fire, pure beeswax and an oil of coconut, olive, or some other benign vegetable, one ounce of each. Add a few fragments of dyed candle wax if any color should be required, and twelve drops of strong-scented oil. Warm all of these until they are well mixed; then pour them out into a small jar or seamless box.

A balm so prepared shall be of great power in ceremonial anointments of the brow, throat, wrists, etc., either before or during the celebration (as may be learned later in this book). The face shall be made fair, the hands strengthened, and the body enlivened by such application, as also any ritual object may be better consecrated if the proper scent be spread upon it. Yet take care that the scent be fitting to the use, one that is warm and sweet for purposes connected with the Sun, cool and sharp for the Moon, dark and heavy for night, or secrecy, and strong and pungent for Earth, new life, etc.

There are also healing properties to a balm of fine substance and fragrance, and for all aches of the body and brain, great comfort can be found in such anointment.

Candles and Incenses

Excellent candles may be made thus: melt beeswax, or paraffin wax, or the wax of Bayberries, over a very low heat. Then stir in a spoonful of some fragrant oil, color the candle as required by adding shavings of drawing wax, and when all these substances are clear and well blended, pour them into a small earthenware vessel, with a depth of two or three inches. This vessel may be made especially for the purpose out of garden clay, and inscribed before it is dry with a sharp knife or twig. Before the wax is poured, a length of sturdy string should be tied to a rod or stick placed across the vessel's rim, so that the string runs straight down through its center. Then pour in the wax, and set the vessel aside for an hour or so, after which the rod may be removed and the wick cut to a proper length.

Long tapers may be bought and used for ritual purposes, but their colors must be carefully chosen—never too pale nor too harsh, and always befitting the ceremonial occasion. They should be anointed with fragrant oils to give them power and spirit, either by hand or by using a small brush of camel's hair.

An incense may be created from any pungent or sweet scented leaves, flowers, or roots, by drying these thoroughly and grinding them to powder in a mortar. Perfumed oils are often added to give strength to this substance. Then it may be burnt in a small brass bowl, or scattered upon glowing coals in a heavy iron cauldron. The rising smoke from this or any incense is of great benefit to all ceremonial occasions, as a symbol of spiritual ascent as well as an inspiration to the senses.

Ceremonial Potions or Libations

During certain rituals, or for other specific purposes or occasions, these spirituous mixtures are offered to good effect. They may represent an abstract quality, or inspire the mind to some significant Awareness, or soothe the body to a state of well-being, according to their concoction and the circumstances of their being taken. Here follow several, of readily procurable components, all first to be well blended before pouring out into some ceremonial goblet or chalice:

One ounce of brandy, two ounces of sweet white port, one teaspoonful of honey—*an excellent libation in rituals of solar import.*

Two ounces of anise cordial, one ounce of Russian vodka, one teaspoonful of white corn syrup—*for lunar rites, unsurpassed.*

One ounce of cherry brandy, one ounce of peach brandy, one teaspoonful of honey, a sprinkling of cumin powder—*for inspiring love or passion.*

One ounce of green mint cordial, two ounces of white gin, one teaspoonful of white corn syrup—*for renewed vision and intellect.*

One ounce of apricot brandy, two ounces of sweet Madeira wine, three drops of almond extract—*for beauty of mind and body.*

One ounce of blackberry brandy, one ounce of sweet red port, one-half teaspoonful of vanilla—*for triumph over death.*

One ounce of apple brandy, two ounces of apple cider, one teaspoonful of honey—*for improved health.*

These potions are of great strength, and should be offered with restraint, lest they overwhelm the sensibilities and lead only to a confusion of their original purposes.

Ceremonial Robes, Shawls, Scarves, Etc.

To surround the body with symbolic beauty is the prime purpose of ceremonial garments. Thus, such clothing should not obscure the flesh, but act as its fitting enhancement and adornment. Choose, therefore, first a soft and close-fitting tunic and hose, or other like garments, dyed to an appropriate color (black may often be used for its neutrality, its suggestion of secrecy, and its harmony with nocturnal rituals) to cover and yet to well reveal the limbs and the bodily form.

Above these, next, various robes, or shawls, or veils, or long scarves, of a soft, thin, even transparent nature should be worn, to spread an ethereal film upon the fleshly contour of the costume. These floating garments may envelop the body from neck to ankle, or cover only the back and shoulders, or even, as with scarves, trail free, attached only at the neck or waist or wrists, but all should be flowing and fine, of fitting color, and sometimes bearing a design or inscription related to the ceremony for which they are worn.

Thus for rituals pertaining to the Sun, there may be small figures of solar import, either words or signs, embroidered in gold thread or inscribed with a gold paint, upon the borders of the robe, with perhaps a gold Sun represented upon the breast. On scarves and shawls also, the borders may be adorned in this fashion, and a significant symbol marked in the center of the cloth.

Scarves should be narrow, the length six times the width, shawls triangular, and large enough to cover the upper arms as well as the back, though they may be worn covering the hair as well. A robe is easily made from two lengths of cloth hemmed at the ends, having a width of four feet, and long enough to reach from shoulder to ankle, sewn together up each side to within eight inches or so of the top, and then joined all across the top save for an opening large enough for the head to pass through. This robe will serve for woman or man, being entirely neutral in design. Yet take care that these thin materials be kept far from the candle flame, lest they take fire and cause their wearer some injury.

Clothing of this sort should be carefully folded and stored away in a chest or box strewn with aromatics such as lavender or shaved orrisroot, that they may keep their power, and endure, and serve you well. Be instructed here that the garments described for certain ceremonies treated later in this book are all conceived according to these directions.

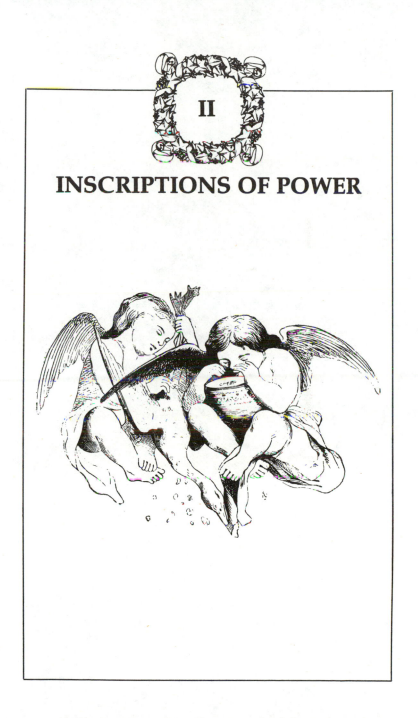

II

INSCRIPTIONS OF POWER

As Words Embrace all things, seen and unseen, so these inscriptions hold within their bounds the essences of what they name. What is invoked exists within its invocation; what is set down is brought to bear on all it touches and on all that surrounds it.

Do not discount the power of such words, nor of the signs and images that well attend them, for they are rich with the wisdom of centuries, and in both ancient and immediate guises they may raise the spirits of their origins, the forces that created them, the world of revelation in which they were conceived.

Thus to call upon the sources whence they have sprung is to summon the strength of their creators—visionary minds, yet also people whose ways were closer to the ways of Earth than ours may be again. The names and images these ancients wrought, for the same elements and entities we still must fashion into life, are potent indeed; and we do well to set them down upon those objects we desire to hallow and empower. As even now we shape words to our purposes, so do these words continue to shape the workings of the Cosmos.

The Inscription of Talismans

The words and images that follow may be set upon various objects presenting themselves to the imagination as appropriate for use as talismans, whether smooth and shapely stones or rocks, blocks or chips of fine grained wood, polished metal disks, leaves of venerable parchment, leather trimmed and burnished, and the like. These objects should be so chosen as to provide two faces. The first, or upper, is to be inscribed primarily with emblems, symbols, or images; the second, or reverse, should bear the words themselves, as covenants and invocations. Such talismans may be displayed openly, yet they are most often kept in secrecy, according to their purpose and appearance. If they are small, they may be carried upon the person to good effect.

Here follow, then, certain inscriptions most fit for their empowering:

For Beauty: Upon the first face of the talisman shall be depicted a small disk with five rays, as a star, flanked by the crescent Moon and fiery Sun. Upon the reverse shall be written, in characters well formed, these words:

> *MORNING STAR*
> *AND EVENING STAR*
> *BY THY LIGHT*
> *I GROW FAIR*

For Dividing Lovers: Upon one face, the crescent Moon enclosing the image of a skull. Upon the reverse, these words:

> *THIS LOVE*
> *THE MOON*
> *DOTH SHRINK*
> *TO BONE*

Against All Sorrow: Upon one face, the head-stone of a grave, bearing a skull. Upon the reverse, these words:

> *SORROW BE DUST*
> *AND DUST DISSOLVE:*
> *LET ALL MY GRIEF*
> *GO INTO THIS GRAVE*

To Gain Wealth: Upon one face, the full rayed Sun enclosing a crescent Moon and three stars. Upon the reverse, these words:

> *YET EARTHLY GOLD*
> *I SOON SHALL HOLD*

For Stability: Upon one face, a skull from which issue the eight legs of a spider, set at the center of a web. Upon the reverse, these words:

> *MY THREADS BIND*
> *THE RESTLESS MIND*

For Eternal Youth: Upon one face, the many rayed disk of the Sun. Upon the reverse, these words:

> *WHO BEARS MY GOLD*
> *NE'ER GROWS OLD*

For Good Fortune: Upon one face, a fair fish curled about the globe of the Earth. Upon the reverse, these words:

> *FLOWERING EARTH*
> *FLOWING SEA*
> *FATTEN, FILL,*
> *AND FAVOR ME*

To Win Healing from the Sun: Upon one face, the disk of the Sun, full rayed. Upon the reverse, these words:

> *MY ORB AND RAYS*
> *GRANT THEE EASE*

To Be Given to Another, for Love: Upon one face, a heart from which flames radiate as from the Sun.

Upon the reverse, these words:

> *MY FIRE THINE*
> *THY HEART MINE*

For Rebirth of the Spirit: Upon one face, a seed of the sunflower, contained within curved stem, leaves, and blossom of this plant. Upon the reverse, these words:

> *OLD SEED, NEW FLOWER,*
> *I BEAR THY POWER*

For Relief from Pain: Upon one face, an eye, rayed with flames as the Sun. Upon the reverse, these words:

> *WHO MEETS MY EYE*
> *HIS PAIN MUST FLY*

For Good Health: Upon one face, a hand from whose fingertips spring flames, as from candles. Upon the reverse, these words:

> *WHO HOLDS MY HAND*
> *MAY HEALTH COMMAND*

To Overcome the Season of Winter: Upon one face, the Sun rayed with alternate flames and leaves. Upon the reverse, these words:

> *POOR SUN, FORLORN*
> *IN WINTER'S GRAVE*
> *ARISE AND BURN*
> *THAT ALL MAY LIVE*

Against Falsehood and Deception: Upon one face, a serpent curled head to tail, encircling an eye rayed with flames. Upon the reverse, these words:

> *THE SERPENT WISE*
> *DEALS DEATH TO LIES*

For Warmth and Well-Being in Winter: Upon one face, the head of a fox rayed with flames. Upon the reverse, these words:

> *NOW THESE TOGETHER RUN RED:*
> *MAN, FIRE, FOX, SUN, BLOOD*

Against Melancholy: Upon one face, wreathed stalks and leaves of the herb Sage. Upon the reverse, these words:

> *OF FRESH SAGE ONE GILL*
> *BREWED IN WATER*
> *CURES MY ILL*

For Immortality: Upon one face, stalks of grass that shed seeds rayed as Suns. Upon the reverse, these words:

> *STALKS BROWN*
> *LEAVES OLD*
> *MY SEEDS*
> *BEAR GOLD*

For Loss of Weight: Upon one face, the Full Moon flanked by crescent Moons. Upon the reverse, these words:

> *WAX THOU MOON*
> *THAT I MAY WANE;*
> *WHAT I LOSE*
> *THEN SHALT THOU GAIN*

For Fertility: Upon one face, an oval egg containing the Sun rayed with flames. Upon the reverse, these words:

> *EARTH AND FLESH NOW ONE*
> *IN THIS EGG, THE SUN*

Against Earthquakes: Upon one face, a stout vine encircling the globe of the Earth. Upon the reverse, these words:

> *NOW EARTH BE FIXED*
> *AND DARE NOT QUAKE*
> *THAT I AND MINE*
> *MAY SLEEP AND WAKE*

For Safety in Traveling: Upon one face, a scallop shell encircled by waves of water. Upon the reverse, these words:

> *EARTH AND WATER BEAR THEE*
> *EARTH AND WATER SPARE THEE*

The Inscription of Amulets

While any amulet may well be worn concealed, the ones recommended in this book are often worn openly, in the manner of decorative necklaces. Having their surfaces exposed to view, they require greater obscurity of language. To this end, only the Latin tongue is used for the words of these inscriptions, and thus a double benefit is obtained—both secrecy, and the tradition of an ancient language in which the words themselves recall elder sources of mystery and power.

As in the inscription of talismans, the first (and outer) face should bear the symbol or image, and the reverse all actual words.

Here, then, follow various inscriptions of power for such amulets as have been described earlier in this book (many of them are well-suited to certain cere-monial occasions of which more shall be written anon):

To Honor the Sun: Upon one face, the Sun rayed with flames, its disk numbered as a sundial and con-taining a central gnomon. Upon the reverse, these words:

> *SOL CUM HOMINE LIGO*
> *UTERQUE CAECUS SOLUS*

For an Invocation of the Moon: Upon one face, the crescent Moon featured as in the human profile.

Upon the reverse, these words:

> *SPECULUM MEUM*
> *FACIES HOMINIS*

To discover the Philosopher's Stone: Upon one face, a Radiant Sun, about whose circumference these words are inscribed: NIGREDO ALBEDO RUBEDO. Upon the reverse, these words:

> *COMMUTATIS EVENIT*
> *AURUM SOLIFERUM*
> *CHRYSOS CHRYSOS*

To Win Love: Upon one face, a winged heart. Upon the reverse, these words:

> *AMOR*
> *VENI*
> *CITO*

Another, for the Same: Upon one face, an open hand with a heart set upon the palm. Upon the reverse, these words:

> *AMOR*
> *TE*
> *TENEO*

To Inspire Passion: Upon one face, the Sun in

flames, enclosing a heart. Upon the reverse, these words:

AMOR TE ACCENDO:
DO TIBI SOLEM

Against Sorrow: Upon one face, a bird, as the phoenix, rising up from flames. Upon the reverse, these words:

DOLOR
NUNC
CINIS

For Improved Health: Upon one face, the rayed Sun enclosing a circlet of green leaves. Upon the reverse, these words:

SIC ESSE
SALUBRIS

To be Safe from all Harm: Upon one face, an eye rayed with flames, as the Sun, containing in its iris a six-pointed star. Upon the reverse, these words:

DEI OMNES
ME SERVANT

To Defy Death by the Power of Life: Upon one face, the rayed Sun enclosing a death's head. Upon the reverse, these words:

>CRAS
>MORS
>HODIE
>SOL

For Wisdom: Upon one face, a serpent curled head to tail, his circle rayed with flames. Upon the reverse, these words:

>SERPENS
>SAPIENS
>SCIO
>OMNE

To Invoke the Sacred Scarab: Upon one face, the Sun rayed with flames, enclosing a beetle, as the scarab. Upon the reverse, these words:

>SCARABAEUS
>SOLIFERUS
>SALVE SALVE

To Celebrate the Season of Spring, as a Source of Fertility: Upon one face, a fountain of water throwing forth leaves. Upon the reverse, these words:

>VER FONS VITAE
>NUNC FLOREO

To Win Power: Upon one face, the Sun at the center of a spider's web. Upon the reverse, these words:

> *OMNE*
> *MIHI*
> *VENIT*

Against Evil Powers: Upon one face, a Crescent Moon at the center of a spider's web. Upon the reverse, these words:

> *POTENTIAE*
> *MALAE*
> *VOS*
> *TENEO*

To Assume the Powers of the Black Sun: Upon one face, the Sun rayed with black flames. Upon the reverse, these words:

> *SOL OBSCURUS*
> *MIHI*
> *POTENTIAE TUAE*

For Eternal Life: Upon one face, a thrice-branched and thrice-rooted tree, its trunk bearing the symbol of Infinity (thus: ∞) while from its three branches rise three flames. Upon the reverse, these words:

> *IGNIS VITAE*
> *FLAGRA*
> *IN AETERNUM*

To be Freed from Habit: Upon one face, the Sun containing a crescent Moon and three stars. Upon the reverse, these words:

> *EGO IPSE*
> *SUM*
> *EXPLETUS*

To Vanquish Death: Upon one face, a death's head having a serpent wound through the eye sockets. Upon the reverse, these words:

> *MORS*
> *TE*
> *MORDEO*

To Invoke the Powers of Sun and Moon: Upon one face, the crescent Moon, extended to form a circle, and this circle rayed doubly with flames and swordlike points. Upon the reverse, these words:

> *AURUM SOLIFERUM*
> *ARGENTUM LUNIFERUM*
> *NUNC HUC ADES!*

To Celebrate Life: Upon one face, the rayed Sun enclosing an eye rayed with flames. Upon the reverse, these words:

> *SOL OMNIPOTENS*
> *TECUM LUCESCO*

Nine Inscriptions for Amulets Honoring and Invoking the Powers of the Nine Stars (Stellae Novem)

I
Sirius, the Almighty

Upon one face, a four-rayed star, colored with four colors about a white center—red, green, blue, and yellow. At its center, the fourth character of the runic alphabet (thus, ᚠ). Upon the reverse, these words:

> *SIRIUS OMNIPOTENS*
> *VERUM FULGENS*

II
Mira, the Wondrous

Upon one face, a four-rayed star of orange color. At its center, the twenty-fourth character of the runic alphabet (thus, ᛜ). Upon the reverse, these words:

> *MIRA MIRABILIS*
> *CREATRIX MIRACULORUM*

III
Algol, the Demonic

Upon one face, a star having four rays of black color, and a white center, within which, the fourteenth character of the runic alphabet (thus, ᛈ). Upon the reverse, these words:

> *ALGOL ANCEPS*
> *DAEMON ET DOMINUS*

IV
Spica, the Spiritual

Upon one face, a four-rayed star of blue color; at its center, the sixth character of the runic alphabet (thus, ⟨). Upon the reverse, these words:

> *SPICA ANIMI*
> *CUSTOS SPIRITI*

V
Antares, the Fleshly

Upon one face, a four-rayed star of red color. At its center, the third character of the runic alphabet (thus, ▷). Upon the reverse, these words:

> *ANTARES GIGAS*
> *IGNIS CORPORIS*

VI
Vega, the Destructive

Upon one face, a four-rayed star of white color. At its center, the tenth character of the runic alphabet (thus, ⍓). Upon the reverse, these words:

> *VEGA VIDUA*
> *FATUM PULCHRUM*

VII
Albireo, the Creative

Upon one face, a four-rayed star of green color. At its center, the seventh character of the runic alphabet (thus, ✕). Upon the reverse, these words:

> *ALBIREO FERAX*
> *VIS VITAE*

VIII
Capella, the Wise

Upon one face, a four-rayed star of yellow color. At its center, the eighth character of the runic alphabet (thus, ▷). Upon the reverse, these words:

> *CAPELLA SAPIENS*
> *VISUS AURIFERUS*

IX
Regulus, the Strong

Upon one face, a four-rayed star of violet color. At its center, the twentieth character of the runic alphabet (thus, ⋈). Upon the reverse, these words:

> *REGULUS RUGITUS*
> *LEO CAELESTIS*

Concerning the powers of the *Stellae Novem*, it may be said that any earthly desire known to humanity must lie beneath the influence of some one of these stars. If the proper one be invoked and honored when it burns in the midnight sky, its fiery being shall radiate all manner of favors upon one who beholds it and wears its name upon the breast.

Two Inscriptions for Amulets to be Worn on a Thong at the Ankle

I
To Walk in Harmony with Earth

Upon one face, the Earth sign (thus, $\oplus$), within a heart. Upon the reverse, these words:

COR TERRAE
COR MEUM

II
To Walk in the Ways of Truth

Upon one face, an eye rayed as the Sun. Upon the reverse, these words:

SIC AMBULO
IN VIAS
VERITATIS

Thirteen Inscriptions Empowered by the Ancient Tongue of Tongues

I
For Riches

Upon one face, the sign of infinity within a four-sided diamond. Upon the reverse, these words:

ZAGIN
ZAGUL
ZAGDU

II
For Fertility

Upon one face, the Sun contained within the Moon. Upon the reverse, these words.

ARGALA
SILMUD
USSA
ARGARGARA

III
Against the Sorrows of Mortality

Upon one face, the Sun containing a triangle, which in turn contains an eye. Upon the reverse, these words:

ARALI
ILUBALAGDI
PIRIG
PIRIG

IV
For Love

Upon one face, the double-curved yoke borne by two Moons, supporting a central Sun. Upon the reverse, these words:

> *AG SUDUN*
> *AG SILA*
> *AG MAH*
> *AG MAH*

V
For Wisdom

Upon one face, an eye within the disk of the Sun, whose rays consist of five leaves alternating with five triangles. Upon the reverse, these words:

> *SILA PIRIG*
> *NAMTAR AGRIG*

VI
Against Evil

Upon one face, a double axe, from each of whose blades depends a serpent. Upon the reverse, these words:

> *ZABIN*
> *NEZAZA*
> *SENTABBA*

VII
To Inspire Passion

Upon one face, a triangle of three equal sides, two of which point downward. Within its center, a spiral, and growing from its upper side, three flames. Upon the reverse, these words:

> *UBUR INNA*
> *ABSIN GALLA*
> *BALAG USSA*
> *IMRIHAMUN*

VIII
For Safety in Travel

Upon one face, a double triangle, set vertically point to point, and behind it curled waters of the sea. Upon the reverse, these words:

> *ZUAB*
> *GARIN*
> *SILA*

IX
For Power

Upon one face, a circle containing at its center a double triangle. As above, each containing an eye, with Crescent Moons set flanking this figure. Upon the reverse, these words:

> *ASTAR*
> *ZAGDU*
> *ARAUNA*

X
To Summon the Dead

Upon one face, a half-circle set horizontally, from which rises a triangle, upon which lies the crescent

Moon on its back throwing forth three flames. Upon the reverse, these words:

ARALI
SILA
ZIGA

XI
For Protection from Fire and Water

Upon one face, a circle from which emanate curled waters of the sea, and within this, the Sun containing the Earth sign. Upon the reverse, these words:

UMU ZUAB
ADDA PIRIG
AG AG AG

XII
To Soften a Hard Heart

Upon one face, a circle with curled waters. As above, containing two triangles pointing one above and one below, between which are set three orbs as of Sun, Moon, and Earth. Upon the reverse, these words:

ASTAR
ZAGDU
ZUAB

XIII
To Invoke the Powers of the Goat

Upon one face, a triangle pointing downward, containing an eye and crowned on its upper side with two curved flames. Also edged on its other two sides with flames, and this whole figure set upon the point of a smaller triangle pointing upward. Upon the reverse, these words:

AZAG
DARA
SANGA

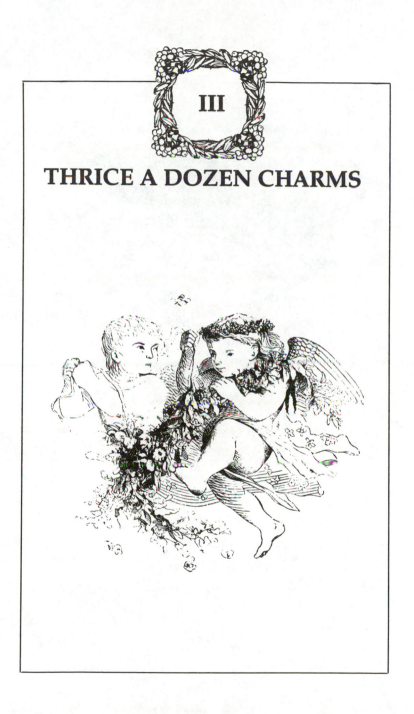

III

THRICE A DOZEN CHARMS

As Has Been suggested within this book before, a charm finds strength not only in its component materials but also in the manner of its fashioning. Therefore do not hasten carelessly to perform what should be slowly and meticulously wrought. The charm will gain Power, as does a seed, most fruitfully where all is well prepared for its unfolding and its flowering. Heed, then, the circumstances, the words of invocation, and the means to best employment of all procedures that shall be here described.

A Charm to Invoke the Powers of the Earth

After rain, when the Earth has received enough of water to be soft, thus clinging to the fingers and to itself, go out and gather up enough to fill the bowl of a large spoon. Bring this into the house, and quickly mold it into a sphere, smooth and rounded evenly. Set it aside in an iron vessel, this covered over with a square of rough sackcloth, and when it shall have dried, after a day or two, remove it and place it in the center of the cloth, with these as well: a small green twig, broken thrice, a soft white feather of down, and a drop of blood pricked from your own finger. Over them, then, speak words to work the enchantment:

> NOW EARTH IS EARTH
> AND EARTH IS AIR
> AND EARTH IS WATER
> AND EARTH IS FIRE:
> LET ALL GO INTO THEE
> AND ALL BE THINE
> LET ALL ARISE FROM THEE
> AND THEN BE MINE

Now fold the cloth to enclose these four entities, and bind it up with a lashing of coarse twine. This charm should be kept in a dark drawer or box, to be taken out and in cupped hands held to the breast, and its words repeated, whenever a strengthening influence is to be called forth.

A Charm to Win the Moon's Aid for a Secret Purpose

A small globe of crystal or clear uncolored glass must first be consecrated by holding it up to the light of the Full Moon, that the lunar image may be caught therein. After this has been performed, the sphere shall serve for a charm to procure the secret wishes of its owner. Thus, on the night of each New Moon, hold the sphere in the left palm, by candlelight, gaze upon it, and say this:

> *CRESCENT BE FULL*
> *AND CRYSTAL FILL:*
> *THUS MY EYE*
> *AND THUS MY WILL:*
> *FIAT VOLUNTAS ABDITA*
> *FIAT VOLUNTAS ABDITA*
> *FIAT VOLUNTAS ABDITA*

The sphere should then be kept in a small bag of leather inscribed with figures of the Moon's phases, and worn tied to a thong about the neck during those days and nights between the crescent and the full. While it is not being worn, this charm should be kept wrapped in a black cloth and hidden away.

A Charm to Win Immortality from the Sun

Find a beetle that takes its shape from the ancient scarab. It were best if it should have a metallic lustre and hue, as of the Japanese beetle that feeds upon the rose. Put it to death by drowning some hours in a tincture of musk and alcohol. Remove it then, and arrange it carefully upon a small cloth of red silk, set in a sunny place, to dry there for three days. After this, the beetle upon the silk should be laid before three gold candles, lighted at midnight, and these words said:

> *SCARAB OF SUN*
> *DARK DEATH IS DONE*
> *GOLD LIFE BEGUN*

Wrap the beetle in the silk, along with a spoonful, each, of these: pollen from the sunflower, rose petals, orris root, salt, and myrrh. Then tie the packet up with a golden thread or ribbon. It should be placed within a small wooden box, which is then sealed with melted beeswax and an image of the Sun inscribed upon its lid. If this charm be kept beneath the pillow for seven days, it shall renew the spirit of anyone who rests the head there. Henceforth, the box should be safely kept and each year consecrated anew, with the same words, before three gold candles at midnight upon the Summer Solstice.

A Charm to Drive Away Evil

Take an iron nail, red-rusted by time and rain, and forged by hand in the ancient form (if such can be found); on a dark night, moonless and cloudy, set down this nail upon a smallish flat stone, and with an iron hammer strike it thrice, at each stroke saying this:

> *CLAVUS FERREUS*
> *MALLEUS FERREUS*
> *FERRUM RUFULUM*
> *FERRUM NOBILIS*

Score the stone thrice across with the nail's point, then take the stone away quickly and bury it in the Earth far from your house. The nail should afterwards be carried with you always, as a charm against evil influences and emanations.

A Charm to Form an Alliance with the Trees

When summer falters before its flight, go on an evening of full moonlight, and cut from an oak tree one true branch, thick with leaves and with acorns bunched. Then, where a wood grows dense and dark, stand at its edge and the oak bough shake—saying these words to the ranks of trees, that their strength may be yours for whatever you please:

> *WITH OAK I LEAD*
> *THAT ASH MAY FOLLOW*
> *ALSO ALDER*
> *ELM AND WILLOW*
> *CEDAR AND LOCUST*
> *HICKORY, LARCH,*
> *WALNUT, CHESTNUT*
> *POPLAR, BIRCH,*
> *BEECH AND MAPLE*
> *FIR AND PINE:*
> *ALL THESE POWERS*
> *SO BE MINE*

Then hang the oak bough over your door, taking one acorn from its store to be sewn up fast in a chamois skin, safe to be kept for what you would win.

A Charm to Rid the Mind or the Body of an Affliction

Gather a quart of water from some spring or stream, and pour it into a large bowl, set within a darkened chamber; by candlelight, then, take a silver knife and write with its point upon the water's surface the name of that which afflicts you. Next, soak a small lock of lamb's wool first in a sweet-scented oil and second in some red wine. Carry it to the bowl and drop it into the water, saying these words:

> *THE DARK BE LIGHTENED*
> *THE HARSH BE SOFTENED*
> *THE RANK BE SWEETENED*
> *BY THE POWER OF THE KNIFE*
> *AND BY THE POWER OF THE WATER*

Leave the lamb's wool there to soak all night, until sunrise, when it should be removed, wrung out, and set to dry upon a small circle of white velvet cloth. Meanwhile, the contents of the bowl should be emptied out into a hole dug in the Earth, and the hole filled in again. When the lamb's wool is quite dry it should be sewn up in the velvet and pinned beneath your clothing, to be worn there for a full month, and thereafter kept elsewhere in safety, that its charmed powers may not be diminished through neglect.

A Charm to Bind an Enemy

Gather from the corners of your chambers every cobweb, and place them, all of a tangle, upon a black cloth. Procure then a fly, recently dead, and set it down upon the mass of webs. These words should then be written down on a paper:

> *NORTH SOUTH EAST WEST*
> *SPIDER'S WEB SHALL BIND HIM BEST*
> *EAST WEST NORTH SOUTH*
> *HOLD HIS LIMBS AND STOP HIS MOUTH*
> *SEAL HIS EYES AND CHOKE HIS BREATH*
> *WRAP HIM ROUND WITH ROPES OF DEATH*

Fold the paper four times, and wrap it up, along with the fly and the webs, in the black cloth, forming a small bag. This should then be bound up with the end of a long cord, and suspended from a hook in some dark corner of the house. Do not disturb it, but let it hang until it is thickly covered with dust. Then it may be taken down and buried in the Earth, to work its influence in perpetual secrecy.

A Charm for Fertility

In early spring, twigs of the alder, bedecked with new red catkins, should be gathered in the first light of morning. Place them in a vessel of water, and set this upon a good-sized mirror near a window where the Sun may fall. Each morning thereafter collect with a feather the grains of golden pollen that have been spilt upon the mirror, and save these gleanings carefully within a folded paper. When no more pollen appears, take what has been gathered and put it into a small bag of yellow silk, along with the same paper, on which these words should be written:

> *POLLICITUM POLLINIS*
> *POLLENTIA POLLINIS*
> *POLLENTIA APPOLLINIS*
> *POLLIS APPOLLINIS*
> *POLLINEM POLLUCEO*
> *POLLEO POLLEO*

Hang up this bag above your bed, and keep it there until a child shall be conceived; then the charm must be burned in a small fire of alderwood, and its ashes strewn over that spot where the catkins were gathered.

A Charm to Transform Death into Life

When it is dark on a summer's night, gather three long strands of ivy where they trail upon stones or trees or the Earth. Bring them into a chamber where one green candle is lighted, and twist the vines into a wreath to fit upon the head. Next, in a mortar crush some white chalk to a powder, and dust the hands and face with a little of this. Then these words should be spoken:

> *WHITE OF BONE*
> *DARK OF SHADE*
> *OF DUST AND NIGHT*
> *MY DEATH IS MADE*
> *DEATH MY SELF*

> *DEATH MY PEER*
> *WHAT I HOLD*
> *I DO NOT FEAR*
> *SO BONE TO FLESH*
> *AND SHADE TO LEAF*
> *DEATH MY DEAR*
> *I GIVE THEE LIFE*

Carefully unbind the strands of ivy, and set their cut ends in a jug of water, leaving them so for two weeks; meanwhile save the crushed chalk that remains. When the time has passed, plant the three ivies at the foot of a large oak tree, and when this is done sprinkle the chalk about them with these words:

> *BONE BE FLESH*
> *SHADE BE LEAF*
> *AS DEATH IS MINE*
> *IT BEARS ME LIFE*

Water and attend these charmed vines faithfully, and they shall give to your present life a strength as the oak's, and to your ultimate death a fruitfulness denying all night and dust.

A Charm to Procure the Heart's Desire

In wet weather walk over the fields, and where the great white mushrooms rise up flat and wide, gather the greatest cap and carry it home. That night, by candlelight, take a large needle and with it scratch this, small, upon the mushroom's upper skin:

> FLESH OF DARKNESS
> BORN OF DEATH
> GIVE MY WILL
> THY LIFE AND BREATH
> WITHER DRY
> AND SHRINK TO DUST
> MY HEART SHALL FEED
> UPON THY CRUST

Breathe upon this inscription, and then lock the mushroom away safely for the rest of that night. The next morning, take a sharp knife and chop the whole into many little pieces. Spread them out in an iron pan and set them in a warm oven until they are quite dry. Then sew them up in a bag of red cloth, and each night thereafter wear this charm over the heart, until the desired effect is accomplished. When it has been fulfilled, the charm should be taken back and buried near the spot where the mushroom was gathered.

A Charm for a Renewal of the Spirit

This shall be done in winter, when leaves are dead and the spirit dark. Bring home from a willow tree that stands by frozen water twelve live wands, stand them in a vessel of water, and feed them with new water every morning until their leaves are born anew from the dormant buds. While these are soft and of a pale green, strip them all from the twigs and with a pestle, in a mortar, pound them to a paste. Spread this out in a shallow dish, set at a sunny window, and when the paste is dry, powder it in the same mortar where it was first prepared. Add some sweet scented oil, a few drops, to this dust, and then, at night, burn it as an offering before twelve yellow candles. While it burns, say this:

ALL THAT WAS DEAD IS NOT DEAD. ALL THAT WAS DARK IS NOT DARK. THE SPIRIT IS A FIRE. THE SPIRIT IS ETERNAL. THE SPIRIT IS ONE SPIRIT—THE SPIRIT OF ALL SPIRITS, AND THAT ONE HOLDS THE FIRE OF THE COSMOS. BREATHE HERE NOW, AND SO SHALL THE COSMOS BREATHE, AND OF ITS OWN BREATH SHALL THE COSMOS BE MADE ANEW.

Save the ashes of the incense in a small wooden box, tied about with threads of gold, and keep it always near as a charm to invoke the influences of the foregoing ceremony all year long.

A Charm for Recalling the Faithless

At midnight light a new black candle in a locked chamber. Take the white wing feather of a dove or pigeon and dip it in some pungent scented oil, rue, wintergreen, or the like. Then let its tip burn in the candle flame, and say these words:

> *THY FLIGHT BE STAYED*
> *THY WING BE BOUND*
> *THIS CLOUD CASTS THEE*
> *TO THE GROUND*

Dip the feather again into the oil, then break it into small pieces and fold these up in a bit of silver paper. Bind this charm with black thread, and bury it in the ground near your doorstep. So shall it call the faithless one back, and when returned, drops of the same oil must be touched to the brow and the palms of that person, who then shall not leave again. Yet reveal not the reason for this anointment, lest its power be diminished.

A Charm to Nourish the Wits and Renew the Powers

You must go in late summer to certain rank stream beds or low pasturelands to seek out the blue vervain, whose flowers are small and near-purple and whose stem is four-sided. Pluck this herb, several stalks of it, and bring these into the chamber where your works are most often performed. Here four candles of violet hue shall be lighted, and an oil of sweet lavender, in a dish, set in readiness. Bare the floor of this chamber, and inscribe upon it in blue chalk a large circle. In its center set the oil and the stalks of vervain, also a good length of black cord. Then step into the circle, and with the chalk write these words small around its inner circumference:

> *VERBENA HASTATA*
> *QUATTUOR ELEMENTA*
> *QUATTUOR LOCI*
> *HASTA VERBENA*
> *VIAM MONSTRA*

Next bind up the stalks of vervain with the cord spiralled about their full length, to make a thick wand. Dip its flowered end into the oil and with it retrace the circle, anointing its boundary well with sweetness. The circle, so charmed, should then be covered up and hidden by a rug or carpet, to be preserved until time shall wear it away, and the wand of vervain hung up over the entrance to this chamber, that it may direct the ways of the one who passes and repasses beneath it. So shall the influence of this ancient herb be fixed there, and the wisdom it conjures arise perpetually in those surroundings.

A Charm to Work Revenge

Gather from the hawthorn tree, or from some great-thorned rose, three thorns of noble length. Set them to steep in an oil of civet, and meanwhile take the heart from a fowl which has been readied for the cooking pot and seethe it in white vinegar over the fire. When the heart is well-boiled, remove it, and put it into the oil with the thorns, to remain there until the last stroke of midnight, at which moment light three black candles, and soon plunge the three thorns into the heart, with each thrust saying one of these:

> *THIS SHAMES THE DEED*
> *THIS BLAMES THE HAND*
> *THIS BLIGHTS THE HEART*

Wrap the pierced heart in a scrap of ragged cloth, and dig for it a grave in some waste place where weeds flourish and rubbish lies strewn about. This charm so buried is most deadly, and shall bring such ruin to its victim that it should not be undertaken without serious consideration of the consequences. The effect may be lessened, and a weaker form of revenge worked upon its object, if the heart, once pierced, be not interred but rather preserved in a small vial of the oil in which it was steeped. Some single misfortune then, and not such dire devastation, shall befall the one in whose name the charm is kept.

A Charm to Win Another's Love

Take of violet blossoms, shorn from their stems, a great handful, and spread them upon a red paper to dry for a fortnight, or longer if need be. When they are quite curled and crisp, grind them in a mortar to dust, and mix this well with two dozen blanched almonds pounded to a paste, and a little clear honey to bind all together. Then from this confection shall several small cakes be shaped. Wrap up each cake closely in silver paper; tie it about with a purple thread, and pack all these sweets into a small box, itself then to be wrapped in silver and tied with purple. When these preparations are completed, set the box upon the same sheet of red paper, on which now a circle has been drawn and these words inscribed in its center:

VIOLA VIOLAE
TINCTUS ANIMAE
CUSTOS LAETITIAE
LENO AMORIS

Turn the box thrice about, raise it thrice in the air, thrice repeat aloud the words written on the paper, and finally kiss the box nine times. Then it may be sent (but secretly, for the identity of its giver should remain hidden) to the one whose love is sought. The inscribed paper should be folded small and kept beneath your pillow, until its purpose is well accomplished.

A Charm to Win Honor and Favor
in the Eyes of Others

Fill an iron pot with fine, dry sand taken from a
bank or pit, but not from the sea, and set it down in
bright sunlight. Then with a lodestone or magnet stir
the sand about, and if it be an Earth of high virtue
certain grains of iron will cling to the lodestone when it
is drawn forth. Remove them into a white bowl, and stir
the sand again to draw further particles of iron from it.
Continue the gleaning until a small spoonful of this
substance has been obtained. Then empty it out upon
the center of a circular piece of red silk, and over it set a
small paper bearing these words written in red ink:

METAL OF STRENGTH
BLOOD OF EARTH

> OUT OF DEATH
> I DRAW THEE FORTH:
> I HONOR THEE
> NOW FAVOR ME.

Tie up the paper, folded, and the iron dust, within the red silk, and wear this charm on a red cord about your neck for twenty-eight days and twenty-eight nights. Then untie it, and pour out the iron into a shallow dish of water. After three days collect the rust that has formed, and with it stain the palms of your hands. This influence will not soon pass away, and should attract warm regard from all whom you encounter.

A Charm to Cure the Body of Sundry Ailments

Take a lump of beeswax as big as your thumb, warm it until it is softened, and fashion it into a human figure. Before a lighted white candle, when the night is dark, hold this figure in the left hand and anoint it with a tincture of aloes. Then dip it into a small bowl of honey, sprinkle it with ground white pepper and with powdered turmeric, and quickly wind it about entirely with a ribbon of white silk, after which it should be wrapped tightly in a small piece of white cloth. Leave it thus before the burning candle for a full hour. During this time, prepare a bath of hot water, and in it dissolve a teaspoonful each of the aloes, the honey, the pepper, and the turmeric. Lie down in this water quietly until it begins to grow cool; then arise, dry yourself, and dress in clothing that is entirely of white. Return to the burning candle, and say these words before it:

> *THE BITTER CURES*
> *THE SWEET CURES*
> *THE SILVER CURES*
> *THE GOLD CURES*
> *THE DARK CURES*
> *THE LIGHT CURES*
> *THE WARM CURES*
> *THE WHITE CURES*
> *THUS AM I RENEWED THIS NIGHT*
> *AND THROUGH ALL OTHERS SOON*
> > *AND LATE*

Blow out the candle, and take the wax figure in its wrappings to your bed, where it should be kept beneath the pillow from that night until two Full Moons have risen. Thus it may serve to charm certain ills from the body, while more baths of the same nature should be taken often for their excellent salubrity.

A Charm to Win Control Over Another

Paint with a brush and India ink, upon a ragged scrap of cloth, the figure of the person you would control. Furl the cloth into a scroll, tie it with a thread of black, and curl this up into a tightly rolled coil. Wrap the coil in a vine leaf, and this in a scrap of red silk, and this in a circle cut from silver foil. Wind it round with red thread, seal it well with sealing wax, and pack it in a hollow walnut shell. Set both halves together tight with glue and then with wax again, and mark this on the nut to fix the spell:

> *NUX NOX*
> *PAX POX*
> *HEX HAX*
> *WIX WAX*
> *HITHERO HOTHERO*
> *WITHERO WOTHERO*
> *WELL*

Shut the nut within a box, bound about by heavy twine, and you shall hold the subject in your rule. So shall he do as you command, a feckless shadow to your hand, though he be fabled king or common fool.

A Charm to Keep a Cat from Straying

To win the faith and affection of a cat, her dignity and overweening wit notwithstanding, you must please her and make her smile. Your way of charming must amuse and entertain her while it takes her fancy and so claims her. Therefore, dry for some days in a clean white bowl thirteen leaves of good unblemished cat-nip—none that has been broken, or trodden, or neglected among weeds, but for preference that which you have planted in a decent corner of the garden—for her pleasure. When the leaves are dry, crush them to powder with a silver spoon, and mix them into a spoonful of fat from some fine hen or duck or goose, or else into an ounce of best butter. When this ointment is stirred smooth, let it rest for an hour or so. Meanwhile, invite the cat to sit upon a table in your kitchen. Set before her a small dish of cream, a few ounces of cooked fish, and a morsel of raw beef, and while she eats them say this to her:

> *GRIMALKIN GRIMALKIN*
> *FEASTED IN MY KITCHEN*
> *THERE SHALT THOU STAY*
> *NOR FROM IT CARE TO STRAY*

When she has finished, stroke her back thrice and collect the hairs of fur that cling to your hand. Fold them up in a paper, and put them in a safe place. Then, kneeling on the floor and holding the cat, anoint her paws with the mixture of fat and catnip. Carry her to your door and set her free then; she shall soon wash her paws with relish and laughter, and her good humor thereafter compliments your deed. Next take the paper in which her fur is folded, and write upon it those same words which were said over her feasting. Seal it up with wax and a seal, and keep it hidden somewhere so she may not find it, thus to bind her in secrecy as well as openly by her consent.

A Charm to Gain Wealth

When a fresh hen has been dressed for the stew pot, save one of its feet and while it is still of a fresh yellow, rub it well with whiskey and with salt. Place within its claws a new silver coin, and also a scrap of paper on which this is written:

HEN HEN
GIVE ME GAIN
THUS TO HOLD
SILVER AND GOLD

Curl up the claws and tie them about with black cord so that all they contain is secure. Then hang this charm by the same cord from some eave of your house, and it shall draw money there within the year.

A Charm to Warm the Affections of Another

When snow falls swift and dry, a cloth of red velvet should be cut into the shape of a heart, as wide as your hand. Go out and stand in a place where the flakes may float down freely, then hold out the heart upon your palm, saying this:

STAR, CRYSTAL
SILVER STONE
I WARM THEE NOW
TO BLOOD AND RAIN
NOR SHALT THOU TURN
TO ICE AGAIN

Return into the house, there breathing upon the snowflakes that cover the velvet until they have melted into drops of water; then fold up the cloth into a triangle and pin it with a golden pin, so to remain while every day thereafter the same words shall be spoken over it anew. When its purpose is accomplished, the next charm should soon be worked to strengthen and preserve its influence, as shall be shown.

A Charm to Bind the Affections of Another

Pluck from the roadside or some neglected plot of ground an old and withered stalk of burdock burrs. Pick off three round burrs, lightly, with cautious fingers, and set them down, each separated from the other, on a table of bare wood. There light three red candles, and carry to them the charm of velvet cloth earlier prepared. Unpin it and unfold it; then spread it flat beside the burrs, and set the three upon the velvet's center, one by one, while these three verses are said:

> *THIS THINE EYE*
> *I BIND TO ME*
>
> *THIS THY HAND*
> *I BIND TO ME*
>
> *THIS THY HEART*
> *I BIND TO ME*
> *EVER AND EVER AND FOREVER*

Move the burrs to lie together, fixed and locked to one another, and likewise all three to the center of the cloth. Then fold up the cloth about them and pin it tight. This charm should then be locked away in a drawer or cupboard, and not disturbed again for fear of loosening its bonds about the one so enchanted.

A Charm to Cause a Proposal of Marriage

To work this charm you should gather twelve red cherries from a tree, or if the cherries must be bought they should soon be washed clean, first in white wine and then in water. Set them in a green bowl, and give them to be eaten by the one whom you would marry. Eat none yourself, but be sure the subject eats them all, and let the cherry stones be saved within the bowl. After he or she has gone away, take the twelve stones and wash them clean; then set them in the Sun to blanch. When they are white and fair, spread them out at night upon a small cloth of red velvet, before twelve red candles. With a fine quill and black ink, mark these words upon them, one letter to each stone:

SPONSALIA MEA

A few drops of sweet scented oil, best of all from flowers of the tuberose, should be sprinkled over the cloth, and then the stones enclosed within it, and the bag thus formed, bound at the neck with red thread. This charm should then be tied onto a gold chain and worn, concealed, as a necklace until a proposal of marriage is called forth. After which it may be undone, and the cherry stones planted in the Earth to ensure that this betrothal be perpetually fruitful.

A Charm to be Given as a Pledge of Love

Procure twelve branches, full berried, from the holly tree, and set them in water between two gold candles, which should be lighted early in the evening and allowed to burn down to their sockets. When they are consumed, pluck all the berries from the branches into a goblet. Then thread a fine needle with a red thread, whose single length shall be twice twenty-four inches, drawing it through the eye until it is double and knotting the ends together. With this needle quickly prick the tip of the fourth finger of your left hand until a drop of blood can be squeezed forth. Anoint the thread with this blood, saying:

> *FRUIT OF RUBY*
> *PEARL OF BLOOD*
> *RED OF LOVE*
> *THY GIFT I GIVE*

Then string the berries onto the thread, taking care not to break them open, and when all are evenly strung together cut free the needle and tie the ends of the thread in a sturdy triple knot. Then this necklace should be hung up near the fire to dry and grow firm. As soon as it is so cured, it should be packed up in a small wooden box with those words said earlier inscribed upon the lid. So should it be given as a pledge of love to another, but with a care, for ill shall befall anyone who gives this token and betrays it before a year has passed.

A Charm to Turn Aside Evil and Ill Fortune

The mountain ash or rowan tree has long been honored for its power against evil forces. It should ever be treated with respect, that its favor be not turned against the one who employs its strength. In late summer, when the tree is heavy with red fruit (the yellow variety is of a weaker influence), seek out one branch that leans toward the south, and shake it gently until it shall let fall four berries. Gather these up, and also take four of the leaves, carry all indoors, and soon build a fire of good birch or apple wood upon your hearth. When the blaze is ripe and golden, cast one of the rowan berries into the flames, along with one of the leaves, saying this:

> *VIRTUE IS MINE, AS OF THIS TREE*
> *BEWARE THE FIRE I CAST AT THEE*

Cast in the second berry, and a leaf, saying:

> *WISDOM IS MINE, AS OF THIS TREE*
> *BEWARE THE FIRE I CAST AT THEE*

Cast in the third, both berry and leaf, saying:

> *POWER IS MINE, AS OF THIS TREE*
> *BEWARE THE FIRE I CAST AT THEE*

Take then the fourth leaf and fruit, and roast them slowly in an iron pot over the fire until they are dried and blackened. Cool them, and wrap their remains in a red cloth, which charm should soon be buried in the Earth near your threshold. Thus it shall protect the house and those who dwell therein from whatever evil emanations might dare to stray too near.

A Charm to Turn Back the Spirits of the Dead

Where the mistletoe cleaves to some living tree, there to feed its many berries, fleshed pale and waxen as the flesh of corpses, you must go in company (for to go alone would be perilous) and wrench from their fastenings a few stems well furnished with white fruit. Carry them home, and spread them out at night upon a table covered with a black cloth. Set at random in their midst five black candles, burning, and at their center a clear glass vessel. Bring then to the table all of these: a red wine of the Medoc, a strained tincture of red carnation petals infused in alcohol, an oil of red storax, and five fragments of bone. Set them down in a row, and speak this incantation:

> *FLESH LACKING BLOOD*
> *BONE LACKING FLESH*
> *SPIRIT LACKING BONE*
> *ARISE AND BE FED*
> *ARISE TO BONE AND FLESH AND BLOOD*
> *THIS NIGHT RENEWED BY MORTAL FOOD*
> *NEVERMORE TO THIRST FOR MINE*
> *NOR ON MY LIVING LIMBS TO TWINE*

Mix in the central vessel the wine, tincture, oil, and bone, and sprinkle a little of this potion over all the sprigs of mistletoe. Then, before cockcrow, bear the vessel, and the sprigs wrapped closely in the black tablecloth, away to a burial ground, where, between two graves, the mistletoe should be laid down gently, unwrapped, and the vessel's contents emptied over it. Pluck five of the mistletoe's berries then, to carry home; but leave all else among the dead, there to find fit surroundings instead of where you dwell. The five berries should be preserved in a small vial of red storax oil, and kept always near at hand to calm and turn back any rash spirit who should presume to visit you thereafter.

A Charm for Eternal Youth

Go to a grove of pines, when the Moon is new, and in the Earth beneath their boughs inscribe a circle, wide as you are tall. Lie down within it, your arms extended to meet the circle's rim, and say these words:

> THE ANCIENT PINE
> IS EVERGREEN
> THE CRESCENT MOON
> MAY NEVER WANE
> THE CIRCLE BOUND
> IS EVER ROUND
> AND SO MY LIFE
> AS LIGHT AND LEAF

Pluck three needles of pine from a green branch, take them home, and wind them tightly round about with a hair from your head and a long green thread. Keep this charm beside your bed, that you may dream of eternity, and each night before you sleep, repeat the words that have conjured youth from the enchanted grove. Ever after, you should wear some token of green—jade, emerald, or other stone, ornament, or article of clothing—in honor of this fair spell now threaded through your life.

A Charm to Reveal Truth among False Appearances

When a young fowl has been roasted and eaten, take the carcass, all its bones, and boil these for six hours until the flesh shall slip away. Further scrub the bones clean, freeing each rib and joint from its fastenings, and then let all lie on a paper in the Sun until they are quite dry and white. When these bones are so prepared, place them in a box of black wood and set it down before a single white candle. Gaze into the flame, while considering earnestly all manifestations of that situation from which you would draw the truth. When all these various aspects have arisen before your eyes, take from the box a bone, and inscribe upon it in India ink one possible truth. Next take others, and write upon them the other truths you have envisioned. Then before the candle set out all the bones in a row, and say this over them:

> *BENEATH THE FLESH OF CONFUSION,*
> *BEHOLD THE BONES OF THAT WHICH IS*
> *TRUE: STILL ALL SAVE ONE ARE FALSE,*
> *AND MUST DECEIVE WHERE THE SPIRIT'S*
> *EYE IS SHUT: YET OPEN NOW THAT EYE*
> *AND THE TRUE BONE SHALL RISE*
> *REVEALED*

Replace the inscribed bones in the box, and also all others that remain unmarked, and shake the box to mix them well. Then with the eyes shut, draw from within one bone, on which shall be written the single truth. If it should bear no inscription, all of the supposed truths are false, and the situation must be studied in a new light after a fortnight has passed. Whatever bone was drawn forth, it should this day be hung from a cord in some window where the Sun will cast its shadow upon an opposite wall. Let it remain there, serving to charm the brain and eye to clear vision thereafter, in all instances of concealment or confusion.

A Charm to Break Some Troublesome Habit

You must take a white egg, and, through small holes made in each end, blow forth the contents from the shell. Plug up one hole with a little softened beeswax, then fill the shell, using a fine funnel, with sour red wine. Carefully seal the second hole with more wax, and in red ink write upon the surface of the shell the name of that plaguing compulsion you would be rid of.

Take this egg in secret then to a place where great rocks cover the ground. Stand there and say these Words:

HALLS OF BLOOD WHERE LIFE HAS FLED
WALLS OF BONE THAT CLOSE ME ROUND
I BREAK THY REIGN, THY YOKE I SHED
I CAST THY POWERS TO THE GROUND

Hurl the egg against a rock so that it shall burst into fragments and the contents be spilt upon the Earth. Then gather up the broken bits of shell, take them home, and grind them to a powder in a mortar. This charmed dust should be kept within a small jar, a pinch of it to be placed upon the tongue and swallowed whenever further treacherous temptations may appear.

A Charm to Assuage Anger and Ill-Feeling

A smooth stone, smaller than your fist, should be sought out in the bed of a clear stream or dug up from the garden's soil. Soak it in a solution of salt and water, scrub it well, dry it in the Sun, and then inscribe upon it these words, in green ink:

NOW ANGER MELT
IN TEARS OF SALT
BE TURNED TO LOVE
BY THIS SWEET SALVE

Lave the stone on every side with the cool sap crushed from seven leaves of stonecrop, until even the inscription has been washed away, and then further anoint it with an oil of verbena. It may then be wrapped in green silk and secreted in some drawer or cupboard used by the one whose anger you would assuage; or, if the anger afflicts you yourself, sleep with the charm beneath your pillow for seven nights, after which time it should be kept concealed in your own drawer or cupboard.

A Charm to Waste Another's Wealth

When the mandrake, known also as May apple, unfolds its leaves over the dark floor of the wood, yet before it flowers or bears fruit, dig up one plant, leaves and stem and root, this last with poisoned humors laden, keeping about it the clod of wet Earth to which it clings. Take all home in a stout bag, and there remove the root, saving the soil, but breaking and casting away both stem and leaves. Wash clean the root's deadly flesh, and let it for a week lie still to wilt somewhat. Then mark upon it, in black ink, the name of the one whose wealth you would destroy (yet let this deed be done for reasons other than mere petty envy, lest your own possessions wilt and fall away as well). Then take the Earth you have preserved, and in a bowl, with a little water, mix it to thick mud; therein plunge the root, covering it over well. Remove it, let this plaster dry, then plunge it in to be again well coated; and still a third time work this plastering, so that the root shall be encased within a triple shroud. Wrap it then in ragged cloths, and keep this charm in darkness until the season when the May apple bears its fruit in that same wood. Go then and pluck one of these little apples, bring it home, and in the presence of the mummied root, taste of the fruit in triumph, scornfully, with laughter, saying:

> *SO MUST HE WASTE AND MOURN HIS LOSS*
> *WHILE I MAY FLOURISH IN HIS SIGHT*
> *A GALL TO HIS AFFLICTED FLESH*
> *HIS DARKNESS MOCKED BEFORE MY LIGHT*

A Charm to Dispel a State of Melancholy

Fill a large earthenware pot with soft dark loam, and over its surface sprinkle seeds of grass, gathered from the fields or bought, if need be, but all of them fat and fertile. Set the pot in a sunny window, and water it each day at dawn, saying these words:

> *OUT OF NIGHT*
> *SHINES THE GRASS*
> *SO MY DARKNESS*
> *NOW MAY PASS*
> *AND CHANGE TO JOY*
> *THAT DRINKS THE SUN*
> *AS GOLD THAT FROM*
> *HIS SIDE DOTH RUN*

When the grass has risen high and put forth good foliage, clip half its number and make of this an infusion within a small teapot, letting the leaves steep in the water for full fifteen minutes. Sweeten this tea with honey, and drink it slowly, meditating upon the Sun that has given life to all leaves, and that same Sun toward which your spirit turns anew. The next morning clip the remaining leaves and hang them to dry in a dim corner. Afterwards preserve them in a small canister, that they may sustain your joy through the days to come, never permitting their solar influence to depart again.

A Charm to Possess Potency and Passion

The dried skin sloughed from the body of a serpent should be procured by two who are betrothed, or if they seek this in vain, a strip of silver cloth may be used instead. Flatten it out upon a table, and cover it thickly with these: dried grass-blades, leaves of tea, leaves of sage, seeds of anise, and a few flakes of hot red pepper. The skin should then be rolled up lengthwise to enclose its contents, and sewed tight with a thread of purple. The long serpent so created shall next be taken and hidden beneath the mattress of the bridal bed, while the lovers recite these words:

> *O SERPENT WISE*
> *THY FLESH DOTH RISE*
> *TO WARM THE BED*
> *WHERE WE SHALL WED*

Then upon the nuptial night, the two shall bring forth this serpent into candlelight and make an anointment of his body with sweet tinctures of musk and ambergris. Then they shall hold him up over a wide bowl or basin, and pull out the thread that binds him together, letting the herbs within fall down into the bowl. These should then be infused in boiling wine to brew a potion, which shall presently be strained clear and drunk slowly. Finally, the two, in nakedness, shall anoint each other entirely with the same tinctures, after which the marriage may be consummated. Thus shall the serpent at last be led to redeem that flesh of mankind which from antiquity, by sustained venoms, he has so slyly betrayed.

A Charm to Increase Beauty

When you may happen upon the split shell of the locust or cicada clinging to a tree, remove it, taking care not to break it in any part, and preserve it in a box. Then when you have need of it, set it forth in a large brass bowl before a gold candle burning, and pour over it these scented oils, a few drops of each: jasmine, tuberose, narcissus, rose, and gardenia. Touch the locust then with the candle flame, setting it afire, and say these words:

> DEAD THING, EVIL, OLD AND DRIED
> THIS FOUL SKIN BE CAST ASIDE
> AND THUS TRANSFORMED TO GOLDEN
>   FIRE
> NEW AND YOUNG AND FINE AND FAIR

When this fire goes out, take the ashes remaining in the bowl and crush them to a paste among the dregs of oil; then tip the candle to drip wax into the bowl, to a spoonful or so, blending this with the other substances while the mixture cools and thickens. All should then be scraped together and formed with the fingers into a ball, this to be wrapped up in fine silk and kept in a drawer near the mirror where your face is most often reflected. Each time henceforth when you look in this mirror, repeat the words of the incantation, and afterwards close your eyes for a dozen seconds before looking again. The beneficial effect shall soon be worked if the words are said slowly, and if the scented charm be passed to and fro before the face while they are repeated.

A Charm to Recall the Dead, in the Name of Love

If it be possible, a letter once written by the one who has died should be found, or else an article of clothing, or picture if a good likeness, or some book, worn from his or her touch. Cut from whatever memento is procured a few corners or shreds to make a spoonful of snippets, and bring these at night, with fine incenses of myrrh and sandalwood, to a table where seven white candles are burning. Sprinkle the snippets over the incense, all contained within a vessel of brass, and then set these alight with one of the candle flames. While they burn, speak these words:

> *THY PRESENCE IN THIS ROOM*
> *DENIES BOTH TIME AND TOMB*
> *THY SHADE BEFORE MY EYES*
> *BRIGHT AS FLAME DOTH RISE*
> *NOR SHALL IT COOL OR PALE*
> *UNTIL MY LIFE MUST FAIL*

When these substances have all ceased to burn, their

ashes should be gathered into a box and the candles left to consume themselves entirely. Soon after this you must buy a new gold locket on a chain of gold, and place within it a pinch of ashes from the box, while repeating the words of the previous ritual. Thereafter the locket should never be opened again, but worn always about your neck to be warmed by the warmth of your own life. Thus shall your devotion confer comfort upon the beloved dead wherever he or she may lie, and likewise that presence upon your breast that shall work your own grief's assuagement. Any ashes that are left within the box may be scattered upon the west wind, where they shall meet that departed but immortal spirit flowing ever toward the Sun.

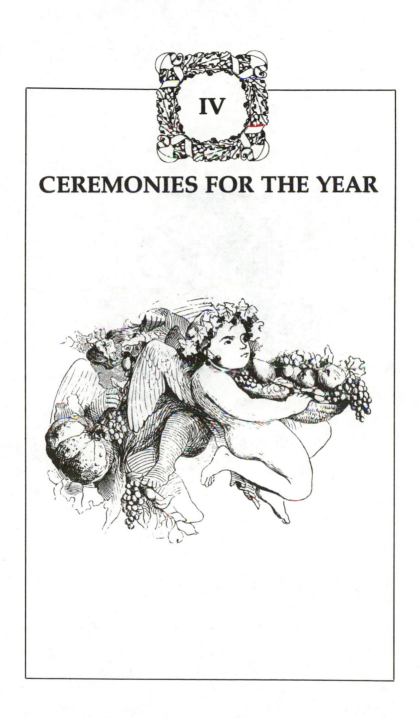

IV

CEREMONIES FOR THE YEAR

Here, Lastly, Shall follow twelve brief symbolic rites, in which some of the foregoing ideas and practices find expression, expansion, and elevation. The complete cycle, moreover, may be seen ultimately to transcend all of its individual parts—about which more will be said presently.

There are no strict requirements for the settings and circumstances surrounding these rituals, save that they be performed in a chamber providing sufficient seclusion, silence, and space for their best realization. Let such a room be as free as possible from furniture and other distracting elements, and see that there be dark hangings at the windows that can be drawn entirely. All doors to the chamber should be closed and even locked.

That which shall serve as the altar may be merely a stout table, great enough to bear all the objects necessary to the ceremony. As will be seen, a cloth of some description covers this altar upon every occasion;

therefore the table itself need not be of great beauty. It may, however, be set upon a low platform if one should be available. Thus its importance, and the significance of what it bears, shall appear the greater. The floor before the altar should be cleared, allowing sufficient space for all celebrants to stand well back from the area where the one who leads the ritual shall be passing to and fro.

The proper time for each ceremony is indicated within its description here, and should be adhered to as closely as possible; however, if this exact time is not convenient, it may be adjusted somewhat, so long as the time substituted is appropriate to the requirements of the ritual. It should also be added that if for some reason the actual performance of these rituals is not possible, they may be read through, aloud or silently, upon the proper occasion, thus to be visualized and contemplated. Their benefit shall even so be gained.

There is nothing of pure invention in these ceremonies, nothing that does not in some way grow out of the unchanging truths of the universe, the solar system, the Earth and its yearly cycle of seasons. Through even these brief rituals it may well be seen how the year and its seasons follow a pattern directly related to the life of human beings, as it may also be said that they live their life according to the great cycle of the year— and this naturally, for they are no less a part of such seasonal events than is the Earth itself.

Earth's long ritual, performed in twelve phases and set in the mode of highest tragedy, is our human ritual as well, and if we follow this course, celebrating in turn each phase of Earth's great truth, we may then also strengthen knowledge of ourselves and of all our life. For out of these twelve phases or fractional truths springs the one great truth—that immutable design of creation, destruction, and rebirth which time does not alter, which continues year after year within even the very spirit of human beings, whether they perceive it or not.

For those who will recognize them, there are comfort and encouragement, as well as inspiration, to be found within these laws. The joy of the creative phase influences even the darkest aspects of the destructive, for when the greater truth enters into its lesser parts, no part is simple or final. Thus we may see death at the center of life, yet likewise life perpetually triumphant over death; and those who live according to this vision shall become, at last, infinitely wise and eternally whole.

A Ceremony for the First Day of the Year

Here begins the new flight of Earth about the Sun, the two risen together anew from the ashes of the past to carry life into the universe again. Out of darkness, into darkness, their light stands here rekindled for another enactment of the eternal cycle.

Before sunrise of this day, in a room facing the east, all its windows heavily curtained, the altar should be prepared. Cover it with a smooth, white cloth. Set three white candles at its center, and before them arrange these three things: a white bowl holding crushed ice, a triangular prism of clear glass, and a mortar full of pure white chalk ground to a dust. At one end of the altar place a vessel containing oil of gardenia, and before it a white bird's feather. At the other end, a clear goblet full of white mint liqueur. All garments worn, robes and the like, should be white, with no embellishment save for a solar amulet which may hang about the neck.

The time of sunrise must be determined beforehand; then, at this moment, the ceremony shall begin.

First light the candle behind the mortar full of chalk, saying:

I AM THE LIGHT OF ALL DAYS THAT ARE PASSED, AND MY NAME IS **PREPARATION.**

Then light the candle behind the bowl of ice, saying:

I AM THE LIGHT OF THIS DAY TODAY, AND MY NAME IS **RENEWAL.**

Then light the candle behind the prism, saying:

*I AM THE LIGHT OF ALL DAYS TO BE, AND
MY NAME IS **REVELATION**.*

When the candles are lighted, the mortar of chalk should be lifted in both hands, and this said:

*ANCIENT EARTH TURNED TO STONE,
WHITENED DUST OF ANCIENT BONE,
PURE AS DEATH, COLD AS SNOW,
DEAD THOU WAST, BUT LIVEST NOW.*

The chalk should then be poured out over the ice, and these words said:

*CRYSTAL CRUSHED, VISION BROKEN,
WATER FETTERED, WORDS UNSPOKEN,
WHAT IS FROZEN SHALL BE WARM,
WHAT IS FORMLESS SHALL TAKE FORM,
WHAT WAS SCATTERED SHALL BE WHOLE,
GIVEN LIFE WITHIN THIS BOWL.*

Then with both hands mix the chalk and ice in the bowl until a milky substance is formed. The fingers so whitened should then be pressed for some moments to the brow of every person present, each time with these words:

*THIS PURIFIES THEE AS IT IS PURE
THIS GIVES THEE LIFE AS IT IS GIVEN LIFE
THE PAST PREPARES THEE
THE PRESENT RENEWS THEE
TO THEE THE FUTURE SHALL BE REVEALED*

The oil of gardenia should then be poured, a spoonful or so, into the palm of the left hand, and an anointment of all three candles performed, thus: dip up this oil with the bird's feather, and brush it over the sides of the candles until the wax is scented and shining, upon which, this should be said:

> WHITE OF PETALS, WHITE OF ICE,
> WHITE OF DUST AND WHITE OF STONE,
> WHITE OF WAX AND WHITE OF GLASS,
> WHITE OF CRYSTAL, WHITE OF BONE,
> ALL THINGS KEEPING, ALL THINGS GIVING,
> OUT OF NOTHING, ALL THINGS LIVING,
> OUT OF EMPTINESS, ALL LIGHT,
> OUT OF BLINDNESS, NOW OUR SIGHT.

The goblet of liqueur should then be held up to each candle in turn, that the flames may shine through it; afterwards, it should be passed for every person to drink, until it is emptied.

The prism should then be raised in both hands high above the head, and these words spoken:

> I AM THE WHITE SUN RISEN OUT OF
> DARKNESS: FROM MY BROW SPRINGS
> ALL LIFE AGAIN AND AGAIN. I AM NOW
> PREPARED, I AM NOW RENEWED, I AM
> NOW THY HOPE, AND THY COVENANT,
> AND THY REVELATION.

The window curtains should quickly be drawn aside, and the prism held up to the Light. If the day be fair and unclouded, the Sun's early rays may be caught in the prism and cast into the room; if there be clouds, the brightest part of the sky should be gazed upon through the prism's side; then also should the feather be held up and gazed upon through the prism, that it may be seen tinged with spectral color. After which, these words should be spoken:

> *THE SUN IS LIVING: HE IS RISEN:*
> *THE WHITE BIRD ASCENDS, AND WE*
>   *ASCEND:*
> *OUT OF THE WHITENED ASHES OF WINTER,*
> *OUT OF THE WHITE STONE AND THE*
> *WHITE CRYSTAL,*
> *OUT OF THE PURE WHITE FLAME:*
> *HIS FEATHERS ARE SCARLET AND THEY*
>   *ARE AZURE,*
> *THEY ARE FIERY, THEY ARE VERDANT,*
> *THEY ARE GOLDEN, AND THEY ARE OF*
>   *ROYAL PURPLE:*
> *HE IS ALL THINGS LIVING,*
> *HE IS THE SPRING AND THE SUMMER,*
> *HE IS THE AUTUMN AND THE WINTER,*
> *HE IS TIME, HE IS REVELATION,*
> *HE BURNS FROM THIS FIRST DAWN*
> *EVEN UNTO THE LAST DARKNESS OF THE*
>   *YEAR*
> *INTO WHICH HE WILL FALL*
> *AND FROM WHICH HE WILL RISE AGAIN*
> *AND FROM WHICH HE WILL RISE AGAIN*
> *AND FROM WHICH HE WILL RISE AGAIN*

Then the prism may be replaced upon the altar, and the

candles blown out, with these final words:

> *THESE GO OUT*
> *BUT NOT THE SUN:*
> *WE DO NOT END*
> *WHAT HAS BEGUN*

So shall the ceremony be brought to its conclusion.

A Ceremony for Mid-February

At the time when one is most weary of winter's cold and emptiness, then shall this ceremony be directed toward the fertile promises of Earth and the warmth hidden in her patient flesh. For she sleeps only, and her awakening has been assured by by the fires of December and by the newly arisen light of January. At the Vernal Equinox will she truly turn to new conception. Yet even now in this spare-seeming month, her substance is complete, her wealth immense, and by proper invocation there may be found a softening in her stony frosts. Call forth then the strength of her darkened seeds, and behold her no longer barren but only bared, soon to be summoned by the Sun of spring.

The altar for this ceremony should be spread with a length of brown velvet. Six candles, colored as the six colors of the spectrum, shall be set in a row, according to the spectrum's order, along the cloth. No incense or scent of any sort should be provided, but all garments worn shall be ornate and fantastical, with flowing scarves and ribbons of gaudy hues, many bright amulets and strands of beads, and rings upon the fingers and the toes (for the feet should be bare). Some budded twigs, rinsed clean and set in an earthen jug of water should be placed at one end of the altar, and at the other a like jug holding new golden ale, with an earthen mug beside it. In the center of the table should stand a large pottery bowl half-filled with Earth dug up that day from the cold garden, and near it a small box of seeds, either of flowers or from any common weed, as burdock, which stands even now in the waste places, full of fertile knots and burrs. The time of day for this ceremony is not important, yet it might best be performed in the early evening following some afternoon of Sun and moderate thaw.

Thus all shall begin—the six candles are lighted, and these words said:

EARTH ASLEEP IN WINTER'S BED,
ON THY LIMBS THIS LIGHT BE SHED,
ON THY FACE AS STILL AS STONE
AND SILENT, DREAMING OF THE SUN:
HE SHALL COME TO CLAIM HIS OWN,
THOU SHALT WAKEN TO HIM SOON
YET TODAY WITH CANDLE BEAMS
WE OURSELVES MAY WARM THY DREAMS.

Each candle in turn should be passed over the bowl of Earth, and then the bowl lifted in both hands, with these words:

FLOWERS OF SUN
FLOWERS OF EARTH
SLEEPING, TURN
TO SHARE OUR BREATH

Set down the bowl and remove the twigs from the jug of water. Hold them over the bowl a few moments, then stand them upright in the jug of ale, saying:

> *NOW MAY THIS GOLDEN POTION OF THE*
> *SUN*
> *FILL THEE WITH SWEETNESS AND A*
> *BRIGHTENED SLEEP*
> *WHEREIN THY DREAMS SHALL WEAR A*
> *BETTER SHAPE*
> *TO SET THEE FLOWERING WHEN THY SLEEP*
> *IS DONE.*

Then take the jug of water and pour it over the Earth in the bowl until all the Earth is moistened. Each person should now bend over this bowl, and breathe upon it thrice, while these words are recited thrice:

> *WARMTH OF OUR BREATH WARM THY*
> *BREATH,*
> *WARMTH OF OUR FLESH WARM THY FLESH:*
> *WE WHO ARE WAKING MELT THY STONE,*
> *WE WHO ARE LIVING THAW THY BONE:*
> *INTO THY SPIRIT WE BREATHE OURS:*
> *OUT OF THY SLEEP WE FATHER FLOWERS.*

Next scatter upon the surface of the watered Earth all the seeds from the box, with these words:

> *SPARKS, STARS, SUNS, SEEDS,*
> *SOON BE RAISED TO GLORIOUS WEEDS,*
> *NOBLE ROSES, SOVEREIGN TREES,*
> *ALL WHOSE STRENGTH BEGINS IN THESE.*

Take then the twigs from the jug of ale, set them again in the other jug, and fill the earthen mug with ale; it should be offered to all present, with this:

> *WHERE LIFE HAS STOOD*
> *THE DRAUGHT IS GOOD*
> *SO DRINK THE BREW*
> *AND LIVE ANEW.*

When the ale is finished all should attend to these words:

> *NOW THE SLEEPER DREAMS HER GOLDEN*
> *DREAM,*
> *BOUND IN WARMTH THAT FLICKERS*
> *EVER BRIGHTER:*
> *YET WE MAY SURROUND HER QUIET BED,*
> *HER LIMBS SHE RESTS IN SUBTLE*
> *NAKEDNESS,*
> *WITH ALL THE GAUDY GARMENTS WE*
> *HAVE KEPT*
> *TO DRIVE DARK WINTER BACK INTO THE*
> *GRAVE.*
> *SHE SLEEPS IN NOTHING BUT HER*
> *FERTILE FLESH*
> *TO SHIELD HER FROM THE WIND AND WIN-*
> *TER'S EVIL,*
> *THEN SHOULD WE HIDE OUR EVERLAST-*
> *ING HEAT*
> *BEHIND THE COLORS OF ALL SPRING*
> *AND SUMMER?*
> *CAST OFF THOSE COVERINGS AND BE*
> *NO LESS PREPARED TO GREET THE SUN*
> *THAN SHE.*

Each one should then take off some articles of bright clothing and ornament, much or little according to inspiration, and all these be piled before the altar as an offering. Say then:

> *THIS IS OUR WARMTH*
> *TO EARTH NOW OFFERED,*
> *THESE OUR FLOWERS*
> *PLUCKED FOR HER TAKING:*
> *WE HER ATTENDANTS*
> *WAIT FOR HER WAKING,*
> *SO WE MAY RISE,*
> *LIKE HER, WELL FAVORED*
> *BY SUN AND HIS STRENGTH*
> *THROUGH ALL HIS REIGN'S LENGTH.*

All should then bend in obeisance over the bowl wherein earth, water, and seeds are contained, each saying:

> *I OFFER THEE ONLY*
> *WHAT IS THINE:*
> *I AM THY SEED*
> *AND THY CREATION*
> *SO MAY I GROW*
> *AND SO REMAIN*
> *THINE IMAGE, SPIRIT,*
> *FLESH, AND VISION.*

The ceremony shall then be ended by each person's breaking a fragment of twig from those in the jug, to keep for a talisman and covenant.

A Ceremony for the Vernal Equinox

As on this day the Sun returns to strength and Earth is roused from her fast sleep, all the signs of her awakening shall proclaim this glad event, and great rejoicing attend their nuptials.

Thus, in the late evening of this day, the altar shall be covered in a fair cloth of bright yellow, and twelve yellow candles be set upon it in a single row. No flowers should decorate the altar, but it is of great importance that many long withes of the willow tree, bound with yellow ribbon into a sheaf, be laid out upon the cloth. A brass bell, incense of sandalwood, oil or a balm, also of sandalwood, a vessel of sweet golden wine, and a goblet, should all be arranged before the candles. As for robes and the like, they shall be all of yellow, light and falling free about the body. Little adornment is desired, other than plain gold rings upon the fingers.

As the ceremony begins, the room should still remain in darkness. The bell is sounded once, and then the first of the twelve candles is lighted, with these words, spoken softly:

> *WHAT IS THIS SOUND*
> *AND WHAT THIS LIGHT,*
> *BRINGING AN END*
> *TO SLEEP AND NIGHT?*

The bell is rung again, and another candle lighted, which two things are thus repeated until all twelve candles have been lit. Say, then, less softly:

> *WHENCE THIS MUSIC?*
> *WHOSE THIS FLAME?*
> *WHO WAKES EARTH*
> *TO LIFE AGAIN?*

The bound willow withes are then grasped firmly in their center, and the cut ends rapped thrice upon the altar; these words shall follow:

> *WHO IS IT KNOCKS,*
> *WHO WOULD COME IN?*
> *SHE KNOWS HIM STILL:*
> *HER LORD, **THE SUN**!*

The incense then is lighted, and oil or balm taken to anoint the hands, arms, and faces of all who attend. Thereafter, this is said:

> *LET HER PREPARE*
> *HER FLESH MOST FAIR*
> *FOR HIS DESIRE*
> *WHOSE FLESH IS FIRE.*

Next one of the candles is carried to the door of the room, and these words spoken:

> *UNBOLT THE DOOR*
> *FOR HE IS HERE:*
> *NOW LEAD HIM FORTH*
> *TO GREET HIS EARTH.*

Open the door, then slowly move back to the altar. Set

the candle down again, and speak these lines:

> *NOW THE YOUTHFUL SUN DOTH ENTER*
> *ONCE AGAIN HIS DEAR EARTH'S CHAMBER:*
> *GOLDEN FLAMES PROCLAIM HER LOVER,*
> *SOFT SHE WAKES BENEATH HIS FERVOR,*
> *STRONG HE SHINES IN AMOROUS FEVER*
> *QUICK TO WIN HER PASSION'S FAVOR,*
> *FIRE TO FIRE THEY CLEAVE TOGETHER,*
> *KINDLING SPRING, CONCEIVING SUMMER,*
> *JOINED FOREVER AND FOREVER*
> *THOUGH DARK AUTUMN COME, AND*
>   *WINTER.*

Take the willows next and undo the ribbon that binds them. The two ends of a single withe should be wound together to form a circlet, and then others likewise fashioned, one to be placed upon the head of everyone present. When this has been done, speak these words:

> *AS WITHIES ARE YELLOW THE WILLOW*
>   *SHALL BRING*
> *GOLD FOR QUEEN EARTH, AND GOLD FOR*
>   *HER KING:*
> *A SHEAF AND A CROWN AND A ROUND*
>   *WEDDING RING,*
> *FOR THIS IS THE SONG THAT THE WILLOW*
>   *DOTH SING:*
> *"O YELLOW THE SUN THAT SHALL TURN*
>   *ME TO GREEN,*
> *AND YELLOW HIS FIRES THAT BURN FOR*
>   *MY QUEEN,*

YELLOW MY BRANCHES THAT MARRY
  THE TWAIN
TILL I WEAVE THEM A CRADLE OF GREEN
  LEAVES AND RAIN.

Then the crowns shall be unwound, and all the wands laid end to end about the floor in a great circle. Let all present now step within this circle, to stand in a ring while this is said:

THIS THE CIRCLE OF THE SUN,
THIS THE CIRCLE OF THE EARTH,
THIS THE CIRCLE OF HIS FLAME,
THIS THE CIRCLE OF HER FAITH.
A CIRCLE OF GOLD, A CROWN OF FIRE,
TURNED TO THE CIRCLE OF THEIR DESIRE.
A PLEDGE OF LOVE, A MARRIAGE RING,
TO BIND THE QUEEN, TO BIND THE KING.

Next a libation of wine should be poured into the goblet and drunk by each person, with these words:

HERE AT THE MARRIAGE
OF SUN AND EARTH
DRINK TO THEM BOTH
ETERNAL HEALTH.

The goblet should be refilled and drunk until the wine is gone. Then all shall say:

BRIDE AND BRIDEGROOM
BOUND TOGETHER,
BIND US TOO
TO ONE ANOTHER.

Half the number of those present shall then each take a Willow withe from the floor and with it encircle the waist of another celebrant, while these words are said:

> *WE ARE THE SUN,*
> *WE ARE THE EARTH,*
> *CIRCLES OF FIRE,*
> *CIRCLES OF FLESH.*
> *SPRING IS OUR MARRIAGE,*
> *SPRING IS OUR BED,*
> *SO IN THIS SPRING*
> *OUR SOULS ARE WED.*
> ***JOINED FOREVER AND FOREVER***
> ***THOUGH DARK AUTUMN COME, AND***
> ***WINTER.***

The couples should then embrace, and the candles be blown out; thus the ceremony is concluded. Any true marriages that arise from this ritual shall be known supremely favored and not easily undone.

A Ceremony for the New Moon in April

When the first crescent Moon of April is setting at evening, go out and gather from the trees some of their small branches, budded or in new leaf. Bring them in and set them in a clear glass jar of water. Then the altar may be prepared.

Cover it with a cloth of bright green, and set two green candles at either end; arrange at the altar's center the jar of branches. A silver goblet and a flask containing green mint cordial mixed equally with white juniper spirits should be placed to one side of the branches, and, on the other side, a green balm of myrrh and vetiver combined. The clothing should be simple, of both green and white, worn with necklace and rings of silver that should be neither weighty nor of crude design. Some small silver amulet bearing the image of the crescent Moon would be most fitting.

The ceremony shall begin with these words:

LUCINA
LUCINA
OCCIDUA
SED NUNC ORIOR
NATIO, NATIO!

Light the candles, and then turn, with the arms held out wide and curved upward, to say this:

CRESCENT LUCINA,
SUNK IN THE WEST,
BORN THIS NIGHT,
MOTHER OF MOTHERS,

MOTHER OF WATERS
MOTHER OF GREEN LEAVES,
CUP OF SILVER, CUP OF GREEN WATERS,
HOLDING THE WATERS OF SKY,
HOLDING THE WATERS OF BIRTH,
HOLDING THE WATERS OF SEA,
HOLDING THE WATERS OF EARTH,
BEAR US THESE LEAVES,
BEAR US THIS SEASON,
BEAR US THE GREEN CHILD
WHO SHALL BE THY CHILD,
WHO SHALL BE OUR CHILD,
WHO SHALL BE OURSELVES.

Next kneel down, and say these words:

THOU WHO ART LUCINA
THOU WHO ART DIANA
THOU WHO ART LIGHT
THOU WHO LIVEST IN DARKNESS
THOU WHO CREATEST
THOU WHO DESTROYEST
THOU WHO CHANGEST EVER
FROM LIFE TO DEATH
AND FROM DEATH TO LIFE,
HIDE NOW THY FACE OF COLD FURY,
READY THY WARM WOMB OF MERCY,
QUENCH THY COLD WHITE FIRE
IN THE WARM GREEN WATERS OF SPRING.
WE SHALL BECOME THY CHILDREN,
THEREFORE BE THOU OUR MOTHER,
NOW IN THE SEASON OF MERCY,
NOW IN THE SEASON OF BIRTH.

Then rise, and take the green balm, to anoint first the candles and next the hands and faces of all present, saying:

APRIL IS EVER A GREEN SEASON,
THE SEASON OF THE GREEN CHILD:
WHO NOW SHALL SEE HIM
SPRINGING FROM THE WATERS OF THE
    WOMB?
FROM THE WOMB OF THE MOON,
FROM THE WOMB OF THE EARTH,
FROM THE WOMB OF GREEN APRIL,
WHO SHALL SEE HIM
WHERE HE SPRINGS FORTH?
HERE HE SHALL BE SEEN,
HERE HE SHALL BE BORN,
HERE HE SHALL BE REVEALED.

Remove the branches from the jar of water, and raise them high for all to see. Then lay them down, tenderly, as with an infant, upon the altar, and say this:

> HERE IS THE MOON'S BABE
> BORN NOW TO ALL OF US.
> HE IS OUR GREEN CHILD,
> HE IS OUR BROTHER AND OUR SON.
> WHAT IS HIS NAME?
> HIS NAME IS GIVEN BY THE EARTH,
> HIS NAME IS GIVEN BY WATER,
> HIS NAME IS GIVEN BY US,
> HIS NAME IS OUR NAME:
> HIS NAME IS **LIFE**.

Here take the jar of water, and with the fingers of the right hand sprinkle drops from it upon the branches. Then turn, holding the jar, and sprinkle further drops upon the face of each attendant, with these words:

> I NAME THEE **LIFE**
> AFTER THIS CHILD
> WHOSE NAME IS ALSO **LIFE**,
> WHOSE MOTHER IS THE MOON,
> WHOSE MOTHER IS WATER,
> WHOSE MOTHER IS THE EARTH,
> WHOSE MOTHER IS EVER THY MOTHER.

Then take the flask of green potion, and fill the goblet. Let each person drink from it, passing it until it shall be empty, and then say:

WE HAVE DRUNK THE GREEN WATERS
  OF THE MOON,
WE HAVE SEEN THE OFFSPRING OF
  HER MERCY.
SHE HAS DELIVERED US FROM THE
  COLD FIRE OF HER FACE,
SHE HAS BORNE US FROM THE WARM
  WATERS OF HER WOMB.
WE ARE HER GREEN CHILDREN,
WE ARE DELIVERED AND BORN
*AND WE ARE GIVEN THE NAME OF **LIFE**,*
AS ALL GREEN THINGS NOW ARE NAMED,
AS ALL THINGS NOW ARE BORN ANEW.

The candles may now be blown out and the ceremony ended. But the branches must afterwards be replaced in the jar of water and carefully kept until their leaves have opened fully, and later withered. Then they should be strewn about some ploughed field, that their substance may continue perpetually fruitful.

A Ceremony for the First of May

For this Ritual of Affirmation, performed best in full sunlight or even out-of-doors, the altar should bear two deep blue candles upon a cloth of paler blue. About the candles a profusion of blue and near-blue flowers should be strewn—the blue violet, hyacinth and grape hyacinth, blue flag, wisteria, periwinkle, forget-me-not, scilla, or any others then in bloom. No incense should be necessary, but the candles may be anointed beforehand with oils of hyacinth and lilac.

Provide also a potion of violets, prepared thus: one day earlier pour boiling water over two handfuls of violet blossoms, to fill a small stone jar, and preserve this mixture in a cool place until shortly before the ceremony. At that time, strain the liquor into a goblet of clear glass, stir into it two spoonfuls of honey until they are dissolved, and so it may be set upon the altar.

The garments for this ceremony should be all of blue, pale, deep, or of various shades, and glittering ornaments of gold, silver, and crystal should be worn as well.

To begin the rites, light the candles and say:

*SPRUNG FROM THE DARK INTO THE
LIGHT, BEHOLD THESE FLAMES OF BLUE.
MOST INNOCENT, MOST INTENSE,
RELEASED FROM THE DEPTHS OF NIGHT,
LEACHED FROM THE PALE BONES OF
WINTER, FORMED IN THE MATRIX OF
EARTH, RISEN IN THE FIRES OF THE SUN,*

*FED BY THE WATERS OF SPRING. NOW
THEY BURN, NOW THEY ASCEND AS
WINGS OF BLUE FLAME, ASPIRING TO
THAT AZURE REALM WHITHER ALL FLESH
ASPIRES, WHERE ALL GROWTH SHALL
FIND ITS PERFECT FORM. YET EVEN NOW
THESE ARE PERFECT: THEY OFFER US
THEIR EXISTENCE AS A SIGN OF PRESENT
PERFECTION, THAT WE MAY BELIEVE IN
THE FLESH EVEN HERE, EVEN BENEATH
THE REALM OF THE SPIRIT WHERE FINAL
PERFECTION MUST DWELL. FOR THOUGH
THEY ASPIRE TO THE HEAVENS, YET THEY
REMAIN MOST EARTHLY: HERE THEY LIVE
AS WE MUST LIVE, IN THE REALM OF THE
FLESH—AND YET THEY ARE PERFECT,
AND TODAY WE CELEBRATE THIS
MOMENT FOR ALL FLESH AS IT STANDS
FOR AN INSTANT BALANCED, POISED
PERFECTLY BETWEEN HEAVEN AND
EARTH.*

The potion of violets should be held up, and these words spoken over it:

*THE SPIRIT OF BLUE VIOLETS
IS THE SPIRIT OF THE FLESH:
EARTH AND SKY TOGETHER BLENDED,
TWO REALMS FUSED AND INFUSED,
OF WHOSE TWO SPRINGS WE MAY DRINK
WITHOUT VIOLENCE TO EITHER
NOR TO EITHER ONE NEGLECT.*

SO MAY WE BE WHOLLY GLAD,
SO MAY WE STAND STILL
WHILE OUR FEET TAKE ROOT UPON
*   THE EARTH*
IN HARMONY WITH FLOWERS AND
*   WITH TREES,*
THE DEEP ROOTS AND THE LONG
*   BOUGHS:*
SO MAY WE STAND WINGED,
FEATHERS SPREAD, WEIGHTLESS
WITH ALL EARTH'S GLORIES
WREATHED ABOUT OUR VEINS,
GARLANDED ABOUT OUR MORTAL LIMBS:
SO MAY WE DRINK THE ELIXIR
OF EARTH AND HEAVEN, AND BE GLAD,
AS WE ARE MORTAL AND IMMORTAL,
FIXED HERE IN MOTIONLESS ASCENT,
TURNED PERFECT IN THIS MOMENT,
PERFECT IN THIS PERFECTION OF
*   FLESH,*
DRINKING THE ELIXIR OF PERFECTION.

All should drink from the goblet, and then stand with arms upraised, while this is said:

THE TREE KNOWS THE SKY,
TOUCHING IT WITH ASCENDING LEAVES:
THE TREE HOLDS THE SKY
LIGHTLY IN GOOD GREEN LEAVES:
AS ITS LIGHT LEAVES DRINK THE SKY
THE TREE BECOMES OUR SPIRIT,
AS NOW THE LEAVES OF OUR SPIRIT
MAY DANCE UPON THEIR BOUGHS OF FLESH.

One of the celebrants should then move to stand before the altar, and the others shall take the flowers from it and wreathe the person with them, fixing their stems into the hair, over the ears, upon the shoulders, about the clothing, and shall last fill the hands with violets. Any flowers that remain may be scattered about the feet, and then these words are said:

> *O MAN WHO STANDEST AS A TREE,*
> *TALLER EVEN THAN ALL THESE FLOWERS,*
> *HOW SHOULD WE NOT WORSHIP THEE*
> *WHOSE FLESH IS THE FLESH OF STARS?*
> *WHERE THOU GROWEST THERE ARE*
>   *GARDENS,*
> *WHERE THOU SHINEST THERE IS SIGHT:*
> *THOUGH THOU FALLEST FROM SUCH*
>   *SEASON*
> *INTO WINTER, INTO NIGHT,*
> *YET THINE ILLS THIS DAY ARE HEALED,*
> *AND THY FAULTS WE HERE DENY*
> *STAND THIS INSTANT HERE REVEALED*
> *PERFECT SCION OF EARTH AND SKY.*

Every person should then touch the head and the feet of the one who stands garlanded, and then, kneeling, receive one of the violets from that person's hands, who shall then say:

> *RECEIVE THIS SIGN,*
> *THE PEFECT FLOWER,*
> *TOKEN GIVEN*
> *OF THIS HOUR:*

THOUGH ITS PETALS
PALE AND WITHER,
WHAT WE WORSHIP
LIVES FOREVER.

All shall then rise, and the candles be extinguished to end the ceremony. Each should afterwards carefully preserve the violet given, for its powers shall not pass away.

VIOLETS

A Ceremony for the Summer Solstice

The Ritual of High Solar Celebration should be performed at true noon upon this day. Even if the Sun should be obscured by unfavorable weather, these rites shall well invoke the spirit of his rays; or, if the Sun does indeed shine, that spirit shall be the more evidently enhanced and glorified.

The altar should be covered with a cloth of gold, and a single gold candle be set upon it. Before this candle should be placed a large brass bowl filled with Earth, having strewn upon its surface some glowing embers of charcoal. Arrange elsewhere upon the altar these things: a vase of bunched daisies and buttercups; a small dish of powdered frankincense and orrisroot,

DAISIES

well-blended; a vial holding tincture of ambergris; a flask of fine brandy and a goblet; and, finally, a long golden ribbon, to which have been tied many small gold bells along its length.

There should also be provided a young tree, slender, yet the height of a man, or some goodly full bough cut from a greater tree, having equal height, and this arranged to stand upright against the altar at one end.

The robes for this ceremony should be of gold, or else of white profusely decorated with gold patterning and solar emblems. Tied to each wrist should be several gold ribbons, near an ell in length, and about the neck chains of gold should hang, or gilded solar amulets, or necklaces of amber, while the fingers should bear many and various gold rings. Each person in attendance should wear upon the head a gilded coronet (fashioned from wire, metallic paper, or other appropriate materials) from the back of which shall hang further gold ribbons like those at the wrists.

Have a small clock that strikes brought into the ceremonial chamber, and shortly before noon all celebrants shall stand waiting, in silence, until it has struck the hour. Following the last stroke, the candle shall be lighted, with these words:

NOW SUN STANDS AT THE YEAR'S ZENITH,
AND HIS MANIFOLD CREATIONS THRONG
* BEFORE HIM: HEAR THEN THEIR*
* WORDS:*

KING OF SEASONS, TOWER OF LIGHT,

TREE OF FIRE, CREST OF FLIGHT,
ETERNAL FLOWER, CROWN OF FLAME,
GOLDEN APEX, SUMMER'S NAME,
SUN OUR RULER, SUN OUR LOVER,
SUN OUR FATHER, SUN OUR BROTHER,
WHERE THOU SHINEST FROM THY THRONE
BURN AWAY OUR MORTAL BONE,
TURN OUR FLESH TO BREATHLESS AIR,
BID US RISE TO MEET THEE THERE:
WHERE OUR SPIRITS SHARE THY REIGN
NOR FALL TO MORTAL LIFE AGAIN.

Cast then a handful of the powdered incense upon the coals, and say:

O SUN, MAY WE LIKE THESE VAPORS,
FREED FROM SUBSTANCE, DRAWN BY
FIRE TO ESSENTIAL SPIRIT, RISE ABOVE
OUR FRAIL AND VULNERABLE
COMPOUNDS, SEEKING THY KINGDOM
OF THE IMMORTAL SPIRIT: FOR ARE WE
NOT THINE HEIRS, FATHERED UPON
EARTH BY THY GOLD RAYS? ARE WE NOT
FIRE OF THY FIRE, KINDLED IN THE SAME
UNIVERSAL DARK? WHEREFORE THEN
SHOULD WE NOT RISE WITH THEE, TO
STAND UPON THY RIGHT HAND, WHERE
ALL THINGS STAND IMMORTAL, WHERE
EVERY SPIRIT BURNS ETERNAL? AND LO,
WE ARE WINGED WITH THE WINGS OF
THY SUMMER, SPRUNG FROM EARTH AS
THY BRIGHT FATHERING RAYS HAVE

*CALLED US FORTH: LO, ON THE FLAMES
OF SPRING HAVE WE ASPIRED
TOWARD THEE, AND ON THE WINGS OF
SUMMER NOW WE RISE, ON THY WINGS
WHO ART THE FATHER OF ALL WINGS:
THY WINGED SPHERE OUR KINGDOM,
WHITHER WE ASCEND, WHERE WE SHALL
FIND OUR IMMORTALITY BEYOND TIME
AND SPACE: THE FIRES OF THY FACE AND
THE FIRES OF THY NAME SHALL BE OUR
OWN TRANSFIGURATION AND
REDEMPTION.*

Then over the coals a little brandy should be poured, and as it burns, these words said:

*NOW WE SHALL ARISE,
NOW WE SHALL ASCEND,
NOW WE ARE ASSUMED
IN THE GREATER FIRE
OF THY GOLDEN SPHERE,
O PERFECT GOLDEN KING,
NEVER NOW TO DIE,
NEVER TO DESCEND,
NOR TO BE CONSUMED:
NOW OUR WINGS ARE FIXED
IN THY HEART OF AMBER,
NOW OUR FACES FIXED
IN THINE EYE OF FLAME,
NOW OUR NAMES RECORDED
IN THIS SINGLE MOMENT,
EVERMORE TO BURN*

AS EVERLASTING BRANDS
UPON THE ENDLESS DARK.

Brandy should be then poured to fill the goblet, and all should drink thereof, while this is spoken, for each:

FIRE OF THE SPIRIT,
ELIXIR OF THE SUN,
FILL US AND PRESERVE US
WHILE WE BURN AS ONE.

Then the tree or bough should be taken and held upright before the altar, that with the tincture of ambergris it may be anointed, trunk and twig and leaf. Then anoint the hands of every celebrant, and let this dialogue be performed between the leader and all the others (who shall ask the questions, the leader answering):

WHAT IS THIS FAIR TREE?
IT IS THE TREE OF SUN.
FROM WHAT LAND DOTH IT RISE?
IT RISETH FROM THE EARTH.
HOW HIGH SHALL IT GROW?
TO THIS MOMENT'S ZENITH.
WHEN SHALL ITS LEAVES WITHER?
NEVER SHALL THEY WITHER.
EVEN IN THE AUTUMN?
EVEN IN THE WINTER.
WHOM SHALL IT RAISE UP?
THOU IT RAISETH UP.
BY WHAT NOBLE POWER?
BY THE SUN'S GREAT FIRE.
HOW SHALL WE ATTEND IT?

CROWN IT AND ADORE IT.
CROWN IT AS A KING?
CROWN IT AS YOURSELVES.
SHALL IT THEN LIVE ALWAYS?
THOU SHALT THEN LIVE ALWAYS.
WHO SHALL GIVE US LIFE?
THE SUN SHALL GIVE THEE LIFE.
YET WHO REDEEMS THE SUN?
THOU REDEEMEST SUN.
HOW DO WE REDEEM HIM?
THY VISION DOTH REDEEM HIM.
WHAT SHALL BE OUR VISION?
WHAT IS SEEN THIS MOMENT.
WHAT IS SEEN THIS MOMENT?
THIS TREE, ADORNED AND CROWNED.

Each person shall then remove the coronet from his or her head, and hang it upon a twig of the tree, also weaving the gold ribbons among its leaves. When all have done this, speak these words:

NOW THE TREE IS LEAVED WITH GOLD,
NOW THE SUN RECEIVES HIS CROWN,
NOW OUR DEATHS ARE LEFT BELOW
AND WE STAND BESIDE HIS THRONE:
WHO CAN SAY THAT WE SHALL FALL
WHEN THE EARTH MUST TURN AWAY?
WHO SHALL MARK OUR MORTAL FATE
ON THE SURFACE OF THIS DAY?
WHO MAY CALL OUR VISION FOLLY
WHILE WE LOOK UPON ITS FACE?
SUN SHALL TURN THE BELLS OF FOOLS

TO GOLD, IN HIS ETERNAL GRACE.

Here grasp the string of bells in both hands, and hold it up for all to see, saying:

FOR AS THE LAUGHTER OF GOLD BELLS
IS A JOY TO FOOLS,
SO THE REIGN OF THE GOLD SUN RINGS
  JOY
DOWN ALL THE SILENT HALLS OF SPACE,
WHERE ONLY THE DEAD DENY IT,
THE DEAD WHO HAVE NEITHER EYES
  NOR EARS:
FOR ONLY WE HAVE SAID, AS FOOLS
  HAVE SAID,
THERE IS NO DEATH, WE SHALL NOT DIE,
YET WHO BUT THOSE WHO SAY SO
SHALL BE CALLED IMMORTAL?
THOUGH GOLD BELLS MAY LAUGH
FOR FOOLS ALONE TO DANCE TO,
YET WHERE IS DANCING IN THE TOMB
OR LAUGHTER IN THE GRAVE?
THEN WEAR THE BELLS OF LAUGHTER,
DANCE THE DANCE OF LIFE,
THAT IN THE SILENT DARK
DEATH SHALL BE MOCKED, AND RAVE.

The bells should be shaken thrice, and then wound among the leaves of the tree. Next say this:

CROWNED WITH GOLD,
WREATHED IN JOY,
ART THOU MERELY
SUMMER'S TOY?

NO, THOU TEACHEST
LAUGHTER HIGHER
THAN THE HALLS
OF DEATH INSPIRE:
THOUGH WE FADE
AND WHILE WE FAIL,
WE MAY LAUGH,
AND LAUGHING, FALL.
WHAT IS WOUND
ABOUT THE SUN
MAY IN NO WAY WISE
BE UNDONE;
THOUGH THE SEASONS
CLOUD HIS REIGN,
STILL WE FIND HIM
FREE FROM STAIN:
FALLEN EVEN
INTO RUIN,
HE SHALL STAND
AS NOW WE SEE HIM:
CROWNED WITH GOLD,
WREATHED IN JOY,
SUBSTANCE DEATH
SHALL NOT DESTROY.

The tree should then be grasped by all, and shaken thrice, that its bells may ring loudly. Then the candle may be extinguished. Afterwards, the tree should be borne away into the midst of a wood, and left there in all its adornment. That place, now sacred, must never be revisited by any of those who accompanied it there.

A Ceremony for Late July

This ceremony, which is performed in recognition of the dark side of the year, should begin well after sunset. The altar is draped with several lengths of the heaviest and richest fabrics, velvets, thick satins, and the like, in various shades of dark red and purple. Six candles of a reddish-purple color should be set upon it, and before them should be ranged a wine glass for each celebrant. On one side place a great jug containing the libation, sweet dark red wine mixed equally with blackberry brandy, having a pinch of ground cumin seed sprinkled on its surface. At the other end of the altar should stand a vase of the deepest red roses, strongly perfumed.

Wound all among these things, also trailing down from the altar, all manner of vines should be arranged—of the grape, of purple clematis, of woodbine, of moonflower, or any others suitably long and leafy. A flask of mixed oils—rose, patchouli, and lavender—should be placed near the vase of roses, and also a small vial of that tincture known as gentian violet.

The celebrants should be clothed in as little as possible, with a few long, thin scarves of purple taking the place of any outer robes on this occasion—some heavy rings, also earrings, of brass or dull gold, and about the neck some amulet betokening passion or fertility, shall be worn for ornament.

Let the candles be lighted to begin the ritual, and these words be said:

WE WHO HAVE ATTAINED ALL LIFE NOW
ASK STILL FURTHER JOY: FOR WHAT IS
SOVEREIGNTY THAT TURNS ASIDE FROM
PLEASURE, WHAT IS POWER THAT IT MAY
STAND STILL AND REST CONTENT?
HAVING FLOWN FROM FLESH TO SPIRIT,
HAVING LAUGHED AT DEATH, SHOULD
WE NOT REJOICE EVEN IN THE REALM
WHERE FLESH AND DEATH PREVAIL?
TURNED INVINCIBLE, WE MAY DESCEND
UPON OUR CONQUERED LANDS AND
CLAIM OUR SPOIL. WHERE WE HAVE
LIVED BEFORE, FIXED TO EARTH, WE NOW
MAY LIVE AGAIN: THUS, WITH NEW
STRENGTH, AS THE LONG VINE THAT
HANGS UPON THE TREE OF LIFE, WE
WIND OUR WISDOM HOME AGAIN AND
SEIZE WHAT WE HAVE WON. NIGHT
SHALL BE OUR DRINKING HALL, NO
LONGER HELD BY DEATH AND HIS DULL
MINIONS: CROWD THEM OUT, THOSE
JOYLESS HORDES WHO WILL NOT LAUGH,
AND POUR THE WINE OF VICTORY! AS WE
HAVE CONQUERED BLOOD, NOW BLOOD
WE SHALL ENJOY!

Here pour out the libation from the jug into every goblet, and let each drink the draught and fill his or her glass again until the face grows flushed, the eye brilliant. While all shall drink, this is to be recited:

*UPON THE HILLS AND IN THE FORESTS
NOW THE TREES AND VINES ARE WARM
AND FULL OF LEAVES: AND LO! THE TREE
OF LIFE, THE TREE OF SUN, IS CROWNED
WITH GOLDEN VINES IN THE WOOD
WHERE WE HAVE HIDDEN IT: HIDDEN IN
THE DARKNESS OF THE GROVE, IT
STANDS WHERE LATE WE SET IT, AND ITS
GOLDEN VINES ARE FULL OF PURPLE
FLOWERS, PURPLE FRUIT: SHALL WE NOT
RETURN INTO THAT GROVE AND PLUCK
THE FRUIT THAT SHOULD BE OURS?
WHEREFORE SHOULD WE WASTE THE
JOYS GREAT SUN HAS GIVEN US, OR FEAR
THE POWERS OF OUR STRENGTHENED
BLOOD? WE ARE THE LIVING GODS,
HEAVEN AND EARTH ARE OURS: LET US
THEN POSSESS BOTH KINGDOMS BETTER
THAN WE KNEW TO DO BEFORE, LET US
LEARN TO DO NOW AS WE PLEASE. FOR
EVEN SUN HAS WEAKENED NOW, HIS
ZENITH FAILS, HIS GOLD MERIDIAN SINKS
AND FALTERS DOWN THE AIR, AND HE IS
LORD OF WHAT HAS BEEN, NOT OF WHAT
IS. BUT WE, BUT WE, ARE LORDS OF
EVERYWHERE: WE RULE THE DARKNESS
AND THE LIGHT, AND WILL DO WHAT WE
WILL. THAT TREE OF LIFE, THAT TREE OF
SUN, UPHOLDS US WHERE WE GRASP AS
VINES AND TAKE THEIR LIMBS OUR
PRISONERS. ALL THINGS WE HOLD, AND*

*WE SHALL NOT RELEASE THE BRANCHES
FULL OF PURPLE FRUIT UNTIL WE HAVE
BEEN FILLED: WE FILL, WE SWELL, WE ARE
THE PURPLE OF THE DEEPEST ROSE, THE
PURPLE OF THE ROYAL VINE, NOW
FILLED WITH WINE AND GROWN AS
GREAT AS ALL THE WHOLE GREAT
UNIVERSE—ITS INFINITE PURPLE FRUIT,
ITS DARKEST FLOWER RIPE, ITS HEAVY
PETALS FOLDED FULL ABOUT THE SUN'S
GOLD HEART. LET US SWALLOW THE SUN,
WHOLE, IN OUR PURPLE UNIVERSAL ORB,
OURSELVES THE COSMIC PURPLE GLOBE
WHERE LO! THE SUN HAS SHRUNK TO
NOTHING BUT A SILVER SEED. LO! WE
HAVE SWALLOWED UP THE SUN, AND WE
EXPAND, WE NOW ENCOMPASS ALL, AND
ALL, AND ALL.*

The flask of oil shall now be passed around to all, that
each may pour out a little into one palm. Then each
shall anoint another, hands and face and limbs, while
this is said:

*LET US GLORIFY OUR FLESH, LET US
CELEBRATE OUR BOUNTY AND THE
SWEETNESS OF OUR FLOWERING. FOR WE
ARE YET THE FLOWERING OF ALL THE
UNIVERSE, YEA, EVEN SO WE ARE ITS
FLESH AND BLOOD AND FRUIT. WHO
SHALL STAY OUR HANDS WHEN THEY
WOULD ACT, AND WHO SHALL STARVE*

OUR MOUTHS WHEN WE WOULD FEAST?
GODS WE LIVE, AND NONE MAY CALL US
MORTAL: SAVE FOR THE DRY AND
LIPLESS MOUTH OF DEATH, BUT WHERE
IS DEATH? WE SEE HIM NOT, WE
RECOGNIZE HIM NOT. EVEN IF HE
SHOULD GNAW THE ROOT BENEATH THE
EARTH, EVEN WHILE HE GNAWS THE
HIDDEN ROOT THAT BINDS THE TREE OF
SUN TO EARTH, THE TREE OF SUN
WHEREIN WE CLIMB AND FEAST ON LIFE,
EVEN WHILE HE GNAWS THE ROOT AND
STARVES THE VEIN, THE FRUIT IS OURS:
AND LO! WE SEE HIM NOT, NEITHER ARE
WE BLIND. IT IS BUT WINE THAT VEILS
OUR EYES, AND WINE IS LIFE, WE ONLY
DRINK WHAT IS OUR OWN: WHEREFORE
SHOULD IT BLIND US? WE SEE
OURSELVES, AND THIS SHALL BE ENOUGH
OF SIGHT. FOR O, SWEET, OURSELVES ARE
SWEET, OUR EVERY SELF AS SWEET AS
FLOWERS AND SWEET FRUIT: WE HOLD
THE WINE OF ALL THE GREAT SWEET
UNIVERSE, AND OF THIS WINE WE DRINK,
WE DRAW ALL SWEETNESS FROM THE
TREE OF LIFE. WHOSE BLOOD MAY THEN
BE DRAINED? DEATH'S BLOOD ALONE,
AND NOT THE TREE'S WHEREIN WE CLIMB
REJOICING. SWEET, SWEET, OUR OWN
DARK BLOOD, AS WE ARE FILLED WITH
LIFE. LET US DRINK UP SWEETEST LIFE

*WITH OUR DARK LIPS, LET US CLEAVE
UNTO THE HEART OF LIFE AND SUCK ITS
JUICE, LET US KISS THE HEART, THE VEIN,
THE HAND OF LIFE WHENCE ALL OUR
HIGHEST SWEETNESS SPRINGS.*

Here each celebrant should kiss the left palm of
another. Then all shall come forward to the altar and
receive on their left palms a drop of the gentian violet,
after which the hand should be clenched and opened
again and the violet marks be allowed to dry. Let these
words next be recited, while each time with the words
"Put out the candles," one candle should be duly
extinguished, until all are dark.

*NOW WE ARE MARKED WITH THE WINE
AND THE BLOOD, NOW WE ARE MARKED
WITH THE FRUIT AND THE FLOWER, NOW
WE ARE MARKED WITH OUR LUST AND
OUR POWER. SO LET THIS MARK BE A
SIGN TO DEATH: THAT LAUGHTER IS
STRONGER THAN MOURNING, THAT
BLINDNESS IS MORE RADIANT THAN
SIGHT, THAT EXCESS IS NOBLER THAN
ABSTINENCE, THAT PRIDE IS STRONGER
THAN MEEKNESS. WE SHALL NOT LIE
WITH DEATH IN THE SOBER GRAVE WHILE
THERE IS LIFE WITH WHOM TO LIE, AND
TO DRINK, AND TO CELEBRATE: BETTER
TO LIE UPON EARTH, DRUNK TO EXCESS
WITH THE GLORIES OF FLESH AND*

BLOOD, BETTER TO KISS AND BE MARKED BY KISSES OF FLOWERING BLOOD, EVEN IF THEY SHOULD WOUND US, EVEN IF THEY SHOULD DRAIN OUR VEINS TO DEATH-WHITE ROPES, EVEN IF THEY BETRAY US AND DELIVER US INTO THE KNOTTED BONE-WHITE BONDS OF DEATH.

WE SHALL DARE EVEN TO PUT OUT THE CANDLES NOW, AND DRINK THE DARK-NESS.

O PUT OUT THE CANDLES, THEN, AND KISS THE DARKNESS OF BLOOD: BUT CALL IT NEVER THE DARKNESS OF DEATH, FOR WE HAVE REFUSED ALL DEATH: CALL IT THE DARKNESS OF LIFE, FOR WE GO BLIND, AND ADMIT NO DARKNESS BUT LIVING DARKNESS.

PUT OUT THE CANDLES NOW, EVEN WHILE WE GROW BLIND, AND WE DO NOT SEE, AND WE INSIST THAT WE WILL NOT SEE.

PUT OUT THE CANDLES, AND WE SHALL EMBRACE THE DARKNESS, WE SHALL IN-SIST UPON DARKNESS, KISSING IN DARKNESS, LIVING FOREVER IN DARKNESS, OUR FLESH AND OUR BLOOD AND OUR WINE AS DARK AS ALL DARKNESS ITSELF.

*PUT OUT THE CANDLES, GIVE US EVEN
THE DARKNESS OF DEATH, THAT WE MAY
MAKE LOVE TO DEATH AND WARM HIM
WITH BLOOD AND WINE, AND COVER HIS
BONES WITH KISSES, AND TURN HIM TO
FLESH AND BLOOD IN THE TYRANNY OF
OUR SWEETEST DARKNESS OF FLESH AND
BLOOD.*

PUT OUT THE CANDLES!

Thus in darkness shall this ritual be consummated, and so ended.

A Ceremony for Mid-August

Near the middle of August, when nights reveal the meteors of Perseus, proceed at sunset to cover the altar with a cloth of pale orange silk. Set thereon five candles of orange color, and to one side of them, in an aged and rusting container, some twigs whose leaves have begun to fade or brown, also stalks of the stinging nettle and of those plants named *Artemisia*, the pale-leaved wormwood. On the other side place a small cup of brown vinegar in which has been mixed some dark and bitter vermouth. Next, in the center of the altar set an earthen bowl full of dust gathered from the roadside, and upon the surface of this dust a long, silver ribbon coiled small.

The garments for this ceremony should be of dusty orange or rust-red. Only one fine silver chain may be worn about the neck, while the hands and feet should remain bare.

First the candles should be lighted, with these words:

NOW SUN TARNISHES, HIS RUDDY FIRE
*   COOLS,*
NOW HAZE AND DARKNESS VEIL HIS
*   RUSTED GOLD:*
SOON STARS WILL TOPPLE DOWN THE
*   HEAVY SKY,*
WILL HEADLONG FALL, FLAIL THEIR RAYS
*   LIKE GIDDY FOOLS,*
FAINTING, DRUNKEN FROM ALL SUM-

MER'S DRAUGHTS,
AND FALL WITH A MUTED CHIME, AS OF
  SAD BELLS THAT FAIL:
NOR ARE THESE STARS, BUT ONLY
  MOTES OF STARS
CAST OUT FROM HEAVEN, WASTED ON
  THE AIR,
TRAILING THEMSELVES TO MERE
  MISTS BEFORE THEY DIE:
SO BLEEDS THE SUN, IN SPARKS OF
  WITHERED DUST,
NOT EVEN SPENDING BLOOD, BUT
  DRAWN TO DROUGHT:
A VOID WHOSE DEEPEST WOUND
  MAY YIELD
NO MORE THAN DRY CHAFF BLOWN
  ACROSS A BLIGHTED FIELD.

The silver ribbon should then be uncoiled from the bowl and held out in both hands, with these words:

OUR GOLDEN GOD SLEW ONCE THE
  DRAGON OF THE DARK
AND LED HIS BRIDE, THE EARTH, OUT
  FROM HER STONY CHAINS:
PROUD HE ASCENDED TO THE SKY'S
  FIXED PINNACLE,
AND NOTHING CROSSED HIS LOVE, NOR
  DARED HIS WINGED FIRE,
YET NOW HER FACE OF WORSHIP COOLS
  TO SULLEN STARS,
NOW FROM THE WAVING SUMMER

FORESTS OF HER HAIR
THE GOLD LEAVES FALL, AND SUDDEN
  SERPENTS WIND THEIR KNOTS
ABOUT THOSE ROOTS, AND VENOMS
  TAINT THE SWOLLEN AIR:
HE FALLS, HE CRACKS, HE WEEPS, HIS
  STONY METEORS SHOWER
DOWN THEIR DUST, COLD AS THE SILVER
  SERPENT'S GLARE.

The ribbon should then be wound about the hands and wrists, and this said:

FOR THE PALE SERPENT HAS WOUNDED
  SUN'S POOR HEEL
WHERE LATE HE FLEW SO FAIR ON
  WINGED FEET:
WELL-HIDDEN IN THE DUST, THAT
  CLEVER TONGUE
FORKED WHETTED WORDS INTO HIS
  GOLDEN FLESH:
DARK WISDOM OF THE DUST, THAT CAN
  BUT KILL,
HOW SHALL WE LEARN TO HEAL THE
  SOVEREIGN ILL?

The ribbon should then be knotted about the left wrist, and these words spoken:

THERE IS NO REMEDY FOR HIM,
  NO REMEDY FOR US,
FOR WE HAVE SHARED HIS GOLDEN
  THRONE, AND WE MUST SHARE HIS FALL:

HIS SOVEREIGNTY NOW RUSTED TO AN
   ARID RAIN OF STARS
PLUMMETS US WITH HIM: WE ARE BOUND
   TO HIM AT THE WRIST,
AND AT THE HEEL, AND AT THE HEART:
   AND WHERE BEFORE
THOSE BONDS WERE GOLDEN WREATHES
   AND GOLDEN VINES,
NOW THEY ARE CRUEL SILVER REINS,
   LEAVING US SILVER SCARS,
NOW THEY ARE COILS OF THE SILVER
   SERPENT, KNOTTED,
   AND GRAY, AND FIERCE.

Take up then the cup with its bitter potion, and let everyone present taste thereof, while these words are said:

DRINK OF HIS FALLEN BLOOD,
ELIXIR VENOM-TAINTED,
DRINK OF HIS TARNISHED WINE,
WHEREIN THE SWEET HAS FAINTED,
AND SHRUNK TO WORMWOOD AND TO
   GALL:
ONE TASTE BRINGS DEATH UPON US ALL.

The ribbon should now be unknotted and spread full length upon the altar. Then the bowl of dust should be taken up and handfuls from it showered over the ribbon, with these words:

DOWN FROM HIS WOUND THE UNIVERSAL
   DUST

FALLS UPON EARTH, AND MEETS OUR
  FURTHER DROUGHT,
WHERE WISDOM CURLS AND GLINTS
  BESIDE THE ROAD
IN SLY CONSPIRACY, AND SCRAWLS ITS
WORDS
FOR ALL TO STUDY, WHO MUST LEARN
  TO DIE:
  O SERPENS MORDAX
  SCIO, CADO, MORIOR

Then every person should stand before the altar and press between the palms first, the faded leaves, next, the sprigs of *Artemisia*, and last, the stinging nettles (that their hurtful mark may be set upon each who attends this ceremony). At the same time, these words should be slowly recited, again and again:

  O SERPENS MORDAX
  SCIO, CADO, MORIOR

Then all shall bow their heads, while the candles are extinguished to end the ritual.

NETTLE

A Ceremony for the Autumnal Equinox

On this first day of autumn, when Sun's weakened reign bends altogether to the sovereignty of darkness, the altar should be shrouded in ragged cloths, faded, and gray with dust and age. No candle should light it, neither should any flower adorn it, save for several dried stalks of old and withered thistles, their heads pale with silken down, held in a common glass jar. An oil or balm of rue, bitter in scent, should be placed at one end of the altar; a thickly smoking incense, heavy and pungent, at the other; and at the center a clock, whose ticking is slow and resonant. Before the clock, set an empty wooden box, drab and scarred, fit only to be cast aside, holding within it an ordinary tumbler of cold water.

All garments must be old, worn and thin, as pale and tattered as can be found, and from the shoulders and the wrists torn rags instead of shawls or scarves shall hang; a veil of ragged gray should cover up the hair. No ornaments may deck the body, nor shall there be any color added to the face, nor sweet scent to the flesh.

At the moment when the Sun has set, stand before the altar and, in a low voice, say this:

NOW THE SUN IS OVERWHELMED, AND
WE ARE LEFT ALONE TO DIE: WITH ALL
THE FADED TREES, THE WASTED
FLOWERS, DO WE ALSO FADE AND WASTE.
OUR BIRTH, OUR YOUTH, OUR PRIME,
OUR PROUD EXCESS, OUR COSMIC FALL:
NOW ENDED ALL, AND WE ARE LEFT

*WITH THE MEAN PRIZE OF POVERTY AND
DULL DECLINE, TO FILL THE SILENCES
BETWEEN THE TICKS OF TIME. WHITHER
FLED OUR STRENGTH AND OUR
ASCENDING LEAVES? WHITHER FLED OUR
LAUGHTER AND OUR FOOLISH BELLS?
WHERE NOW STAND THOSE
SCAFFOLDINGS OF FIRE, THOSE LIMBS OF
LIGHT WHEREON WE CLIMBED, WHEREIN
WE PLAYED? ALL ARE NOW PULLED
DOWN, OUR LEAN POSSESSIONS SHRUNK
TO FILL A LITTLE BOX: AND ALL OUR
SENSES, OUR DELIGHTS, TURNED PALE
AND LEACHED OF TASTE, PALED TO A
SCENTLESS DRAUGHT THAT RUSTS THE
HEART TO A MERE FOOLISH TICKING
CLOCK.*

All should then be silent and attend to the sound of
the clock. After a short time, this shall be spoken
softly, thrice over, in rhythm with the ticking:

> *THE BRAIN
> MUST BREAK
> THE BONE
> MUST CRACK
> THE BLOOD
> MUST CLOT
> THE HEART
> MUST STOP
> THE FLESH
> MUST ROT.*

Following this, all shall anoint their hands and faces with the oil of rue, and kneel upon the floor, with bowed heads, while this is said:

> *WE ARE THE STRICKEN,*
> *DYING OF DEATH,*
> *SHROUDED IN WEEDS,*
> *WRAPPED IN OUR LOSS:*
> *SILENT WE WAIT,*
> *CLOUDED BY TEARS*
> *TORN BY THE WIND,*
> *RAGGED WITH MIST:*
> *WHERE WE ARE WOUNDED*
> *THERE IS NO HEALING,*
> *WHERE WE DECAY*
> *NOTHING IS SOUND,*
> *RAVAGED BY NIGHT,*
> *ABANDONED BY DAY,*
> *SILENT WE WAIT,*
> *SHADOWS OF GRAY:*
> *OLD IN OUR BROKEN*
> *HOUSES OF FLESH,*
> *OLD AMONG RUINED*
> *PILLARS OF SUN,*
> *OLD AS THE HALLS*
> *TO WHICH WE DESCEND,*
> *OLD AS THIS DARK*
> *THAT DOES NOT END.*

Then let the tumbler of water be taken from the wooden box, and each person shall drink a little thereof, as this is said:

> *ELIXIRS FADE*
> *AND POTIONS FAIL,*
> *THE GOLD IS RUSTED*
> *FROM THE GRAIL,*
> *THE WINE IS CHANGED*
> *TO WATER THIN,*
> *THE BLOOD IS WASTED*
> *FROM THE SKIN,*
> *AND ALL THAT FROM*
> *THIS GLASS IS DRUNK*
> *MAY LEAVE US ONLY*
> *SMALLER SHRUNK.*

Then the jar of thistles shall be held up and this said over them:

> *EVEN THE KING*
> *GROWS OLD AND WHITE*
> *WHEN ROYAL NOON*
> *HAS TURNED TO NIGHT:*
> *YET BETTER THE PEACE*
> *OF THISTLEDOWN*
> *THAN POWER UNDER*
> *A THORNY CROWN.*

Crush the thistles then into the wooden box, with these words:

> *LET HIM SLEEP*
> *HIS SLEEP OF GRAY*
> *WHERE GOLD AND PURPLE*
> *FALL AWAY,*
> *AND LET US LIE*

> *BESIDE HIM HERE,*
> *PAST PAIN OR JOY,*
> *DESIRE OR FEAR.*

One celebrant shall cover this box of thistles with the veil from his or her head. Then that person shall come before the altar and say:

> **SHALL THERE BE NO ALTERNATIVE?**
> **NEITHER RECOURSE NOR CHOICE?**

Another shall answer:

> *THE CHOICE IS SLEEP OR MADNESS: GO*
> *THEN, SLEEP THAT GRAY AND SILENT*
> *SLEEP THAT COMES BEFORE THE SILENT*
> *DARK, WARMED ONLY BY THE POOR*
> *DOMESTIC FIRE, THAT LEAN AND*
> *FLICKERING FLAME LIT UPON THE*
> *MORTAL HEARTH TO COM FORT MEN IN*
> *AUTUMN: FOR IT MAY WARM, IF NOT THE*
> *SPIRIT OR THE HEART, AT LEAST THE*
> *CHILLY FINGERS YET AWHILE.*

The first shall ask then:

> *ARE THESE NOT THE WORDS OF SOME*
> *GRAY SERPENT FLICKERING IN THE*
> *DUST? WOULD IT NOT BE BETTER TO GO*
> *MAD AND RAVE, TO COURT THE FAIR*
> *ILLUSION OF A GREATER FIRE?*

This shall be the answer:

> *DEATH IS DEATH, AND EVEN MADNESS*

*SOON SHOULD PLAY US FALSE. BETTER
TO SLEEP, BETTER TO CLOSE THE
CURTAINS TIGHT AGAINST THE
TREACHEROUS LAUGHTER OF THE
MOON, AND SLEEP WITH YET A LITTLE
FIRE ON THE HEARTH: THEN WHEN THE
LAST TONGUE FLICKERS AND IS GONE,
THE SLEEPER KNOWS IT NOT. GO NOW
AND SLEEP.*

Thus shall the ceremony end, and all depart. The box of thistles later should be taken to some hearth fire, to be burned until only its ashes shall remain.

THISTLE

A Ceremony for the Full Moon in October

This ceremony is to be performed at night, although not so late as midnight. The altar should be spread with a silver cloth, and four silver candles set upon it. At the altar's center should stand numerous goblets, ringed about a black iron pot containing a block of ice and a large silver ladle. Before the pot set four vessels, each holding one of these: a pale white wine, a colorless cordial of anise flavor, white syrup of corn, and a clear extract of bitter almonds. At one end of the altar set a silver vase containing some naked twigs from the wild cherry tree, some dry stalks of burdock bearing numerous burrs, and a few briar canes, thorny and leafless. At the other end a round mirror, ten inches or so across, should lie upon the cloth, and beside it, these: a small silver bell, a spool of silver thread, and a small vial of jasmine oil.

The robes for this ceremony should be black, edged with silver and inscribed with designs of the Sun, Moon, and stars, all in silver. All manner of silver, diamond, or crystal ornaments should decorate the hands, wrists, neck, and ears, and silver ribbons may bind the hair. Even the eyelids and nails of the fingers should be silvered, and a single brilliant may be fixed at the center of the brow.

To begin the ceremony, the candles should be lighted and the silver bell rung four times. Then let this be said:

HOW SHOULD WE CEASE FROM DYING
AND FROM SLEEP WHERE WE HAVE

*TAKEN REFUGE IN DEEP SILENCE? DOTH
DEATH ALREADY ROUSE US WITH HIS
MUSIC? NO, DEATH HAS NAUGHT TO DO
WITH BELLS OR MUSIC. THIS IS A SILVER
SOUND, A GHOST OF SOUND, AN ECHO
OF SOME LAUGHTER WE HAVE KNOWN—
YET WHERE IS LAUGHTER, NOW THAT
SUN IS GONE? THIS IS THE SOUND OF
LAUGHTER CHANGED TO STONE, AND
WARMTH TO FROST, AND FIRE TO
REFLECTION: O FEARFUL GHOST! IT IS
THE SILVER MOON WHOSE MIRROR
TURNS OUR DEATHS UPON THEMSELVES:
AS THE TRAPPED CREATURE GNAWS HIS
CAPTIVE FLESH, WE WAKEN INTO FRENZY
WHILE WE DIE.*

Let the mirror then be held up above the head for all to
see, and these words recited by all:

*SPIRIT OF NIGHT,
SPECTRE OF SUN,
SCOURGE OF THE DYING,
DOOM OF THE LIVING,
EGG OF THE SERPENT,
WEB OF THE SPIDER,
SERVANT OF DREAMS,
LAMP OF DELUSION
BEACON OF EVIL,
BEARER OF POWER,
CRYSTAL OF KNOWLEDGE,
MIRROR OF MADNESS*

> *ART THOU REDEMPTION?*
> *ART THOU DAMNATION?*
> *SHALL WE ADORE THEE?*
> *SHOULD WE ABHOR THEE?*
> *BRINGEST THOU VISIONS*
> *OF ANGELS OR DEMONS?*
> *SHALL WE REJOICE WITH THEE IN THIS*
> *   AWAKENING?*
> *OR SHALL WE FLY FROM THEE TO KIND*
> *   DEATH'S COMFORTING?*

Take the jasmine oil and anoint the candles, and also the hands and brows of every celebrant, saying:

> *WE LIVE AGAIN*
> *AND WE ARE FAIR!*
> *THE MOON HAS RISEN*
> *HERE TO BEAR*
> *A MIRROR FOR*
> *OUR ALTERED FACES,*
> *AS THEIR FADED*
> *FLESH SHE CHOOSES*
> *FOR HER LOVE*
> *THAT ALL THINGS SEIZES.*
> *WE ARE RISEN*
> *IN HER LIGHT,*
> *WHERE THE DYING*
> *LIVE AGAIN,*
> *THESE RAGS MADE WHOLE*
> *AND REARRANGED*
> *IN PATTERNS OF*
> *HER GHOSTLY CHANGE:*

> *WHAT DULLED AND GRAYED*
> *HER LIGHT MAKES GLITTER,*
> *ALL OUR SENSES*
> *WEAR HER SILVER:*
> *SILVER SERPENT,*
> *SILVER SPIDER,*
> *ALL SHOW FAIR*
> *WITHIN HER MIRROR.*

Then over the ice in the iron cauldron, pour the contents of all four vessels, and stir them with the ladle to concoct the lunar libation, saying this:

> *NOW HER GIFT OF FINE CONFUSION*
> *SHALL BE STRENGTHENED IN THIS POTION:*
> *DRINK IT, THAT HER COLD ILLUSION*
> *MAY REDEEM THY MORTAL VISION.*

The mixture should be ladled out into goblets for all to drink. After it has been consumed, this should be said:

> *COLD HER KISS THAT BREAKS THE BRAIN*
> *TO SNOW, BUT FAIR HER EYES WHERE*
> *FIRE IS WHITE AS CRYSTAL, AND FAIR HER*
> *BROW WHERE SWEET FORGETFULNESS*
> *BREAKS AS A SUNRISE, WHILE SHE KILLS*
> *THE SUN. WE DID NOT CHOOSE HER*
> *MADNESS, WE WERE CHOSEN: YET WHO*
> *WOULD NOT PREFER IT TO THE DARK?*
> *WE KNEW NO MORE OF REASON EVEN*
> *THERE THAN NOW WE DO, WHERE TRUTH*
> *IS SO ADORNED BY HER ELABORATE*

*THREADS AND CRYSTALS, WOVEN ABOUT
ITS FORM, THAT WE FORGET ITS FORM:
BETTER HER MOST DREAD
HALLUCINATION THAN EMPTY SLEEP
WHERE NOTHING SHINES NOR DANCES,
BETTER HER DANCE OF DEATH, HER
PANIC THROES, HER TARANTELLE, THAN
STILLNESS IN THE GRAVE, AND THOUGH
HER MUSIC LEADS US ONLY THERE WE
FOLLOW GLADLY ALL HER DREAD
DIVERSIONS.*

Then take the spool of silver thread, and tie its end to the silver bell. Let one person hold the bell tightly, while the thread is unreeled and wound about all other celebrants, back and forth among them, crossed and recrossed, until an irregular tangled web is formed, binding each within its pattern. Then say these words:

*BOUND IN THE SILVER WEB, BE FREE;
DYING IN FORMLESS FLAME, NOW LIVE;
MADDENED WHERE MADNESS IS A JOY,
FEARFUL WHERE FEAR IS RESURRECTION,
HOLD THOU FAST TO THIS FRAIL THREAD
UNTIL THE LAST FALSE LIGHT BE SHED.
O MOON, FAIR GLORY, GHOST, AND
    GHOUL,
WHAT MATTER IF WE BUT FEED THY EVIL:
ART THOU NOT A BEAUTEOUS BEAST,
AND ARE WE NOT BETTER FOR BEAUTY
    STILL?
LET US AT LEAST BE WELL-BETRAYED*

AND LED TO DEATH BY SILVER SINGING
RATHER THAN SOFT DISPASSIONATE
  NIGHT
WHERE NO STING BLINDS,
NO PAIN ASTOUNDS, AND EVEN
IN ANGUISH, NO VOICE SOUNDS.

The bell shall then be rung continuously, while the silver thread is retraced among the celebrants and thus rewound upon its spool. The candles should finally be extinguished, but the bell should still ring until the last light is gone. Then shall the ceremony end.

A Ceremony for the Dark of the Moon in November

For this ceremony, the altar must be covered with a plain black cloth of dull texture. Upon it set a single black candle, a large, flat, dark stone, a stick of white chalk, an incense burner containing some sharp-scented incense unlighted, a box of ointment having a similar scent, and, finally, the whitened bone of an animal, this wrapped in a piece of black velvet. All garments worn must be of black entirely, with no adornment or decoration save for an amulet, bearing a death's-head, about the neck. A black shawl or hood should cover the head and shoulders of every person present.

At midnight the ceremony shall begin. First light the candle, then say these words:

THE YEAR GROWS DARK
IN THE DARK OF THE MOON:
THE MIND GROWS DARK
IN THE DARK OF THE MOON:
NIHIL STAT
NIHIL STAT
NIHIL STAT
EVEN THE NIGHT IS DEAD
NOW AT THE DARK OF THE MOON:
EVEN THE DEMONS ARE DEAD
NOW AT THE DARK OF THE MOON:
ALL WHO ONCE LIVED ARE DEAD
NOW AT THE DARK OF THE MOON:
NIHIL STAT
NIHIL STAT

NIHIL STAT
WHAT SHALL REMAIN?
THIS SHALL REMAIN!

The bone should be quickly unwrapped and raised in both hands, to be contemplated in silence for several moments. Then these words are spoken:

BENEATH THE EARTH, BEHOLD THE KINGDOM OF THE DEAD: THE PLACE OF DARKNESS WHERE NO WORD IS SPOKEN, NOTHING MOVES: AND THERE THE KING OF DEATH SITS ALWAYS ON HIS CARVED BLACK THRONE, SITS THERE SILENT AND UNMOVING, FOREVER AND FOREVER, A RULER NEVER CHALLENGED, NEVER DISOBEYED: A FIGURE CARVED FROM BONE, HIS FACE THE FACE OF SILENCE, CARVED OF DEATH'S OWN SUBSTANCE WHICH IS BONE, HIS EYES BLACK SHADOWS OF SILENCE, EMPTY CAVES OF BONE. HE SITS UNMOVING, WHILE HE RULES ABSOLUTELY BY HIS SILENCE THE VAST HORDES OF THE DEAD, THOSE SILENT DOCILE HORDES RANKED ENDLESSLY BENEATH THE EARTH, SILENT FIGURES OF OBEDIENT BONE. ONLY ONE LAW RULES THEIR KINGDOM: AND IT IS CARVED DEEP UPON THE THRONE WHERE SITS ETERNALLY ITS MAKER AND ENFORCER: A SINGLE LAW, AND ONE THAT IS NOT BROKEN WHILE THE KING

OF DEATH RULES SILENTLY FOREVER AND
FOREVER: CARVED IN THE STONE ABOVE
HIS SILENT AND UNMOVING HEAD,
*THESE WORDS: **THOU SHALT NOT LIVE**.*

The stone should then be raised by one celebrant for all to see, while with the chalk another shall write these same words upon it: ***THOU SHALT NOT LIVE***. Then all shall chant this song of mortality:

NOR SHALL WE LIVE,
WE WHO STILL LIVE:
HOW SHALL WE LIVE
WHERE HE IS LAW?
OUR LIFE IS DEATH,
A DOWNWARD PATH
INTO THE EARTH,
WHERE EVERY BREATH
WE DARE TO BREATHE
IS A FAREWELL:
IS A FAREWELL:
IS A FAREWELL:

The stone should now be replaced upon the altar, and the incense lighted, with these words:

LET US THEN PRAISE THEE, DEATH,
FOR THY LAW WHICH IS LAW,
FOR THY POWER WHICH IS PROVEN,
FOR THY SILENCE WHICH IS UNBROKEN.
THOU ART PAST ALL SORROW AND
*   REMORSE,*
THOU ART PAST CHANGE, AND CHALLENGE,

AND FAILURE:
THOU ART PERFECT, AS DARKNESS IS
  PERFECTION,
THOU ART PERFECT, WHILE LIGHT MAY
ONLY FLAW,
THOU ART PERFECT, AS ALL ELSE IS
  IMPERFECT,
AS EVEN MIGHTY MADNESS IS IMPERFECT—
WHICH WE HAVE LEARNED, HAVING
OURSELVES BEEN MAD—
AND SUN AND MOON ARE ONLY FLAWS
THAT FLARE AND FADE UPON THE PER-
  FECT SPHERE
OF THY ETERNAL SPACE AND TIME:
LET US THEN PRAISE THEE, DEATH,
LET US ADORE THY FLAWLESSNESS
WHICH SHALL BECOME OUR OWN
  PERFECTION
WHO ARE IMPERFECT NOW,
WHO SHALL YET BECOME MOST PERFECT
  IN THY LAW.

The candle should now be anointed with the ointment, and the hands of all present anointed also. Then say:

SHALL WE NOW PUT OUT THE CANDLE?
SHALL WE NOW PUT OUT THE CANDLE?
SHALL WE NOW PUT OUT THE CANDLE?
THERE IS NOTHING LEFT TO LIGHT,
NOW AT THE DARK OF THE MOON,
NOTHING TO PRAISE BUT DEATH'S
  KINGDOM,

DEATH'S PERFECT UNIVERSAL DARK,
WHERE THERE IS NO NEED FOR LIGHT.
AND THERE WE SHALL BE MADE PERFECT,
THERE WE SHALL LEARN ALL THINGS,
WHERE THERE IS NO NEED FOR
*   KNOWLEDGE:*
NOR NEED WE SPEAK A SINGLE WORD
*   AGAIN,*
NOT EVEN EVER MORE FAREWELL:
NOT EVEN EVER MORE FAREWELL:
NOT EVEN EVER MORE FAREWELL.

The candle should then be lifted from the altar, and blown out. Thus this ceremony is ended, as here the death of the year is made final and manifest.

A Ceremony for the Winter Solstice

This ceremony bears the greatest significance of all during the year, resolving as it does the paradox of death and subsequent rebirth. So shall it be performed with utmost solemnity, yet also with highest rejoicing.

At some time before one o'clock in the morning of this day, the altar should be spread with a bright red cloth of rich material, such as velvet or heavy silk. Twelve red candles should be arranged in a circle at its center. In their midst set a golden basin full of ashes. At one end of the altar place a vase holding holly sprigs, fresh and full-berried, mixed with sprays of juniper and cedar; and at the other end, a flask of young red wine, with goblets sufficient for all who will attend the ceremony.

The robes should be also of red, but at the inception of the ceremony these should be covered up as much as possible by a wide black shawl or long cloak, worn over the head as well. All ornament and all decoration of the clothing should be of gold, but likewise worn well-hidden as the ceremony begins.

When it is just one o'clock, the leader of the celebrants should be waiting outside the closed door to the ceremonial chamber, cloaked as has been prescribed, holding a lighted golden candle in a brass candlestick, and a bell of brass. The leader shall then ring the bell once, and one of the celebrants within the still darkened chamber shall say:

WHO WAKES US FROM ETERNITIES OF
NIGHT?

The leader shall reply:

> *A STAR, A STRANGER, SENT TO BRING*
>   *THEE LIGHT.*

Some other, within, shall say:

> *NO LIGHT OF THINE CAN RAISE OUR*
>   *FALLEN SUN,*
> *AND WE ARE DEAD, BECAUSE HIS LIGHT*
>   *IS GONE.*
> *THY LIGHT AS WELL MUST DIM FOR WANT*
>   *OF BREATH,*
> *YET ENTER: SHARE OUR DARKNESS, AND*
>   *OUR DEATH.*

The door shall be opened, and the leader shall enter, bearing the candle before them. The others now say:

> *THOU BRINGEST HERE AN UNFAMILIAR*
>   *FLAME—*
> *NOW TELL TO US THINE ORIGIN AND NAME.*

The leader shall answer thus:

> *IF THOU COULDST SEE BEYOND THE*
>   *WINDOW THERE,*
> *MY LIKENESS AS A BEACON WOULD*
>   *APPEAR:*
> *I LIVE IN REGIONS FAR BEYOND THY SUN—*
> *THE STAR THOU CALLEST **SIRIUS** IS MY*
>   *HOME.*
> *THE GREAT SUN **SIRIUS**! WHO, THOUGH*
>   *A STAR*
> *TO THY SHORT VISION, FLUNG FROM*

HIM SO FAR,
STANDS SUN OF SUNS, AND MONARCH
*　　TO THY KING.*
SO BY HIS MIGHT, HE SENDETH ME TO
*　　BRING*
THIS FRAGMENT OF HIS LIGHT, A LITTLE
*　　SPARK*
TO KINDLE THEE FROM SLEEP, AND
*　　FROM THE DARK.*

Another shall say next:

RETURN UPON THY WINGS OF FOREIGN
*　　FIRE,*
AND TELL THY KING THAT WE ARE PAST
*　　DESPAIR:*
OUR BONES ARE BARE, NO WARMTH
*　　FROM THEM MAY GROW.*
WE ASK NO GIFT, NOR KNOW TO USE
*　　ONE NOW.*

The leader shall reply:

BUT IF YOUR SUN SHOULD BURN AND
*　　LIVE AGAIN,*
WOULD HE NOT RAISE YOU WITH HIM TO
*　　HIS THRONE?*
THIS LIGHT I BEAR, THOUGH BUT A
*　　CANDLE GLEAM,*
REVEALS TO THEE THE VISION I HAVE SEEN:
THY SUN IS LIVING STILL! NOR DID HE DIE:
HIS STRENGTH IS ONLY HIDDEN FROM
*　　THIS SKY,*

> BUT WHERE I WATCH, FROM **SIRIUS'S**
>   FLAME,
> I SEE HIM BURNING EVERMORE THE SAME.
> NONE DIE BUT THEE, AND ONLY BY THY
>   WILL
> CAN AUTUMN WOUND, AND BITTER
>   WINTER KILL.
> I BRING THEE VISION, FIRE, AND THIS
>   WORD:
> THAT FROM HIS ASHES, LIKE A WAKENED
>   BIRD,
> SHALL SUN LEAP UPWARD, BEARING ON
>   HIS WINGS
> THE HUES OF EVERY EARTHLY BIRD THAT
>   SINGS.

Another shall then ask:

> IF THIS BE SO, HOW SHALL WE SEE HIM
>   RISE?

The leader shall answer:

> THIS MOMENT, ON THIS DAY, BEFORE
>   THINE EYES!

The leader shall then advance to the altar, and taking up a handful of ashes from the basin, scatter them over the unlit candles, after which, with his own candle, lighting the others. Then, setting the golden candle down before the circle of red ones, he should throw back his black cloak to reveal the red robes beneath, and exultant, say this:

*BEHOLD NOW **SIRIUS**, SUN OF SUNS,*
STAR OF THY STARS, THOUGH IN MY SKY
THOU ART INVISIBLE: YET I DESCEND IN
THE GUISE OF FLESH, BEARING TRUTH,
TO SUCCOUR SUCH AS YE, POOR ASHEN
CREATURES SUNK TO MADNESS AND TO
SLEEP. THOUGH I AM COSMOS TO THY
DUST, RADIANCE TO THY SHADOW,
NOON TO THY NIGHT, STILL THOU ART
THE CHILDREN OF THY SUN, AND HE IS
YET MY KIN, THEREFORE ART THOU
FLESH AND BLOOD OF MINE AS WELL,
AND THUS I GIVE THEE HERE MY GIFT,
MY VISION: INFINITE SIGHT, WHEN THOU
WERT DOOMED TO BLINDNESS; LIGHT,
WHEN THOU WERT DEAD WITH
DARKNESS; WINGS, WHEN THOU HAD
THOUGHT ALL WINGS UNFEATHERED,
FALLEN, FAILED. RISE UP THEN,
CHILDREN OF THE SUN, RISE TO HIS
DAWN, REBORN, AND FEATHERED IN THE
COLORS OF HIS INFANT FIRE: FOR WHAT
WAS TRUE AT NOON IS TRUE AS WELL AT
NIGHT: THE UNIVERSE IS EVER AN
IMMORTAL PHOENIX, WHOSE DEATH IS
BUT HIS BIRTH: NOR IS THE EARTH AN
EXILE FROM HIS BREAST, WHERE HE
SPREADS BURNING WINGS ACROSS ALL
SPACE: WHERE HIS RADIANCE EXPANDS,
THERE DWELLS ALL DUST: FLAWED,
FALLEN, MUTABLE, YET STILL IMMORTAL

THROUGH ETERNITY, DYING EVER, YET
NO LESS THE FLESH FROM WHENCE
SPRINGS LIGHT: AND WHERE THE
DARKNESS CEASES, WHERE EVEN ONE
POOR MOTE OF DUST SHALL FLAW THE
SPHERE OF SILENCE, THERE MAY GROW
SOME SUN, SOME EARTH, AND FAIREST
*LIFE. AND I, **SIRIUS**, BURNING EYE OF*
SPACE, SEE ALL OF THESE, AND GIVE TO
THINE OWN EYE ALL THAT I SEE. RISE
THEN WITH ME, RISE TO THE IMMORTAL
PHOENIX I PROCLAIM, AND TAKE OUR
RADIANCE FOR THINE OWN.

Then all shall fling aside their dark cloaks and stand revealed in equal glory. The wine shall next be poured, and all shall drink while this is said (as it once before was said at the ceremony for the Summer Solstice):

NOW WE SHALL ARISE,
NOW WE SHALL ASCEND,
NOW WE ARE ASSUMED
IN THE GREATER FIRE
OF THY GOLDEN SPHERE,
O PERFECT GOLDEN KING,
NEVER NOW TO DIE,
NEVER TO DESCEND,
NOR TO BE CONSUMED:
NOW OUR WINGS ARE FIXED
IN THY HEART OF AMBER,
NOW OUR FACES FIXED

IN THINE EYE OF FLAME,
NOW OUR NAMES RECORDED
IN THIS SINGLE MOMENT,
EVERMORE TO BURN
AS EVERLASTING BRANDS
UPON THE ENDLESS DARK.

Then the leader, as **SIRIUS**, shall say:

REMEMBER ALWAYS THIS:
THAT DARKNESS BENDS TO LIGHT,
THAT DEATH IS ONLY FLIGHT
ALONG THE CURVE OF SPACE:
AND EVERY SWORD OF ICE
IS YET A CRYSTAL FAIR
THAT BREAKS THE BODY'S FIRE
TO COLORS STILL MORE CLEAR:
THEN LIVE REDEEMED FROM FEAR,
AND WHEN THOU SEEST ME
THY WINTER'S CRYSTAL STAR,
A COVENANT, THOUGH FAR
FROM ALL THAT WE SAY HERE,
REMEMBER HOW THIS DAY
I RESURRECT THE YEAR,
AND END THY DEEP DESPAIR:
FOR FLAME AND FURTHER FLAME
BREAK FORTH FROM ALL THAT SEEMS
TO DIE, BUT IS NOT DEAD—
THOUGH BLOOD AND FLESH BE SHED,
BY THIS ALL FIRES ARE FED.

Then the others should recite these words, spoken

also at the Summer Solstice:

> *WHAT IS WOUND*
> *ABOUT THE SUN*
> *MAY IN NO WISE*
> *BE UNDONE;*
> *THOUGH THE SEASONS*
> *CLOUD HIS REIGN,*
> *STILL WE FIND HIM*
> *FREE FROM STAIN:*
> *FALLEN EVEN*
> *INTO RUIN,*
> *HE SHALL STAND*
> *AS NOW WE SEE HIM:*
> *CROWNED WITH GOLD,*
> *WREATHED IN JOY,*
> *SUBSTANCE DEATH*
> *SHALL NOT DESTROY.*

Then shall the leader take up the gold candle, still lighted, bow to all, and go out, leaving the door open. The others may soon follow, but the twelve red candles should be left to burn down until they are consumed. So this ceremony ends, and the universal cycle is renewed.

STAY IN TOUCH

On the following pages you will find listed, with their current prices, some of the books and tapes now available on related subjects. Your book dealer stocks most of these, and will stock new titles in the Llewellyn series as they become available. We urge your patronage.

However, to obtain our full catalog, to keep informed of new titles as they are released and to benefit from informative articles and helpful news, you are invited to write for our bi-monthly news magazine/catalog. A sample copy is free, and it will continue coming to you at no cost as long as you are an active mail customer. Or you may keep it coming for a full year with a donation of just $2.00 in U.S.A. ($7.00 for Canada & Mexico, $20.00 overseas, first class mail). Many bookstores also have *The Llewellyn New Times* available to their customers. Ask for it.

Stay in touch! In *The Llewellyn New Times'* pages you will find news and reviews of new books, tapes and services, announcements of meetings and seminars, articles helpful to our readers, news of authors, advertising of products and services, special money-making opportunities, and much more.

The Llewellyn New Times
P.O. Box 64383-Dept. 892, St. Paul, MN 55164-0383, U.S.A.

• • •

TO ORDER BOOKS AND TAPES

If your book dealer does not have the books and tapes described on the following pages readily available, you may order them direct from the publisher by sending full price in U.S. funds, plus $1.00 for handling and 50¢ each book or item for postage within the United States; outside USA surface mail add $1.50 per item postage and $1.00 handling per order. Outside USA air mail add $7.00 per item plus $1.00 handling per order.

FOR GROUP STUDY AND PURCHASE

Because there is a great deal of interest in group discussion and study of the subject matter of this book, we feel that we should encourage the adoption and use of this particular book by such groups by offering a special "quantity" price to group leaders or "agents".

Our Special Quality Price for a minimum order of five copies of CRONE'S BOOK OF WISDOM is $20.85 Cash-With-Order. This price includes postage and handling within the United States. Minnesota residents must add 6% sales tax. For additional quantities, please order in multiples of five. For Canadian and foreign orders, add postage and handling charges as above. Credit Card (VISA, MasterCard, American Express, Diners' Club) Orders are accepted. Charge Card Orders only may be phoned free ($15.00 minimum order) within the U.S.A. by dialing 1-800-THE MOON (in Canada call: 1-800-FOR-SELF). Customer Service calls dial 1-612-291-1970 and ask for "Kae". Mail Orders to:

LLEWELLYN PUBLICATIONS
P.O. Box 64383-Dept. 892 / St. Paul, MN 55164-0383, U.S.A.

THE WOMEN'S SPIRITUALITY BOOK
by Diane Stein

Diane Stein's *THE WOMEN'S SPIRITUALITY BOOK*, is a work of insight and a much needed addition to women's magic and ritual. Beginning with "Creation and Creation Goddesses" she enthusiastically informs the reader of the essence of women-centered Wicca, using myths and legends drawn from a variety of world sources to bring her work to life. Non-patriarchal myths and tales intersperse the first half of the book, which leads the reader through the yearly progressions of rituals in some of the most complete descriptions of the Sabbats ever published.

The second half of the book is a valuable introduction to visualization, healing, chakras, crystal and gemstone magick. Subsequent chapters cover "transformational tarot" and Kwan Yin.

Diane Stein's *WOMEN'S SPIRITUALITY BOOK* is a tool for self-discovery and initiation into the Higher Self: a joyous reunion with the Goddess.

0-87542-761-8, 300 pages, 6 x 9, illus., softcover. $9.95

THE WITCHES' QABALA—The Goddess and the Tree
by Ellen Cannon Reed

There is a tree that has its roots in heaven . . . a tree that contains all that is, and was, and will be, and might be, and could be. On it, *in* it, are meditations that can, when properly applied, bring about specific spiritual experiences, and solve spiritual problems. It bears on its branches a guide for spiritual growth. It bears the Goddess in all Her Beauty, and the God in all His strengths. It contains a system for training the mind, making the proper astral contacts, guiding your own spiritual growth, or that of others, step by step. It contains a method for helping you and others experience the Mysteries.

This system, so long spurned by paganfolk, can serve all of them well, even with only the most basic knowledge of the subject. The author has brought the two schools together, showing how the religious aspect of the pagan paths may be developed and served by the techniques inherent in the Qabala.

0-87542-666-2, 160 pages, 5¼ x 8, illus., softcover. $7.95

THE MAGICAL HOUSEHOLD
by Scott Cunningham and David Harrington

Whether your home is a small apartment or a palatial mansion, you want it to be something special. Now it can be with *The Magical Household*. Learn how to make your home more than just a place to live. Turn it into a place of life and fun and magic. You will learn simple magical spells that use nothing more than items in your house: furniture, windows, doors, carpet, pets, etc. The result is a home that is safeguarded from harm and a place which will bring you happiness, health and more.

ISBN: 0-87542-124-5, illustrated, paper $7.95

THE WOMEN'S BOOK OF HEALING
by Diane Stein

At the front of the women's spirituality movement with her previous books, Diane Stein now helps women (and men) reclaim their natural right to be healers. Included are exercises which can help YOU to become a healer! Learn about the uses of color, vibration, crystals and gems for healing. Learn about the auric energy field and the Chakras.

The book teaches alternative healing theory and techniques and combines them with crystal and gemstone healing, laying on of stones, psychic healing, laying on of hands, chakra work and aura work, color therapy. It teaches beginning theory in the aura, chakras, colors, creative visualization, meditation, health theory and ethics with some quantum theory. 46 gemstones plus clear quartz crystals are discussed in detail, arranged by chakras and colors.

The Women's Book of Healing is a book designed to teach basic healing (Part I) and healing with crystals and gemstones (Part II). Part I discusses the aura and four bodies; the chakras; basic healing skills of creative visualization, meditation and color work; psychic healing; and laying on of hands. Part II begins with a chap ter on clear quartz crystal, then enters gemstone work with introductory gemstone material. The remainder of the book discusses, in chakra by chakra format, specific gemstones for healing work, their properties and uses.

0-87542-759-6, 6" x 9", color plates, softcover. **$12.95**

THE KWAN YIN BOOK OF CHANGES
Diane Stein

The Kwan Yin Book of Changes places the ancient Chinese *I Ching*, a divinatory system much a complement to the tarot, in a context that women and men in touch with peace can relate to. The patriarchalism and rigidity of the traditional *I Ching* is exchanged for a women-only communal government and world, with situations and language relevant to modern occult women and to men who relate to the feminine aspects of themselves. The God/Emperor of traditional translations is replaced by the im-manence of the Earth and the Goddess, and fate and predistiny give way to free will and choice. The Superior Man of the old versions is the Superior or Spiritual Woman in a system much more positive than any earlier *I Ching* translation.

As a divinatory took, *The Kwan Yin Book of Changes* returns the Chinese *I Ching* to women's use, and is a tool of great power simple to use. The book stands the *I Ching* side by side with the tarot as an aspect of women's spirituality, and is a remembering of the submerged skills of women's matriarchy and culture.

0-87542-760-X, 256 pages, 6 x 9, illus., softcover. **$9.95**

MAGICAL HERBALISM—The Secret Craft of the Wise
by Scott Cunningham

In Magical Herbalism, certain plants are prized for the special range of energies—the vibrations, or powers—they possess. Magical Herbalism unites the powers of plants and man to produce, and direct, change in accord with human will and desire.

This is the Magic of amulets and charms, sachets and herbal pillows, incenses and scented oils, simples and infusions and anointments. It's Magic as old as our knowledge of plants, an art that anyone can learn and practice, and once again enjoy as we look to the Earth to rediscover our roots and make inner connections with the world of Nature.

This is Magic that is beautiful and natural—a Craft of Hand and Mind merged with the Power and Glory of Nature: a special kind that does not use the medicinal powers of herbs, but rather the subtle vibrations and scents that touch the psychic centers and stir the astral field in which we live to work at the causal level behind the material world.

This is the Magic of Enchantment . . . of word and gesture to shape the images of mind and channel the energies of the herbs. It is a Magic for *everyone*—for the herbs are easily and readily obtained, the tools are familiar or easily made, and the technology that of home and garden.

This book includes step-by-step guidance to the preparation of herbs and to their compounding in incense and oils, sachets and amulets, simples and infusions, with simple rituals and spells for every purpose.

0-87542-120-2, 243 pages, 5¼ x 8, illus., softcover. **$7.95**

CHARMS, SPELLS AND FORMULAS
by Ray Malbrough

Hoodoo—a word many have heard, but few have understood. Hoodoo magick is a blend of European techniques and the magic brought to the New World by slaves from Africa. Hoodoo is a *folk magic* that can be learned and easily mastered by anyone.

In this book, Ray Malbrough reveals to you the secrets of Hoodoo magick. By using the simple materials available in Nature, you can bring about the necessary changes to greatly benefit your life and that of your friends. You are given detailed instructions for making and using the *gris-gris* (charm) bags only casually or mysteriously mentioned by other writers. Malbrough not only shows how to make gris-gris bags for health, money, luck, love and protection from evil and harm, etc., but he also explains how these charms work.

He also takes you into the world of *doll magkick;* using dolls in rituals to gain love, success, or prosperity. Complete instructions are given for making the dolls and setting up the ritual.

Hoodoo magick can be as enjoyable as it is practical, and in this fascinating book you can learn how to be a *practitioner*, working your spells and charms for yourself or for others. Learn the methods which have been used successfully by Hoodoo practitioners for nearly 200 years, along with many practical tips for dealing with your clients.

0-87542-501-1, 192 pages, 5¼ x 8, illus., softcover. **$6.95**

THE LLEWELLYN ANNUALS

Llewellyn's MOON SIGN BOOK: approximately 400 pages of valuable information on gardening, fishing, weather, stock market forecasts, personal horoscopes, good planting dates, and general instructions for finding the best date to do just about anything! Articles by prominent forecasters and writers in the fields of gardening, astrology, politics, economics and cycles. This special almanac, different from any other, has been published annually since 1906. It's fun, informative and has been a great help to millions in their daily planning.   **State year $3.95**

Llewellyn's SUN SIGN BOOK: Your personal horoscope for the entire year! All 12 signs are included in one handy book. Also included are political and economic forecasts, special feature articles, and lucky dates for each sign. Monthly horoscopes by a prominent radio and TV astrologer for your personal Sun Sign. Articles on a variety of subjects written by well-known astrologers from around the country. Much more than just a horoscope guide! Entertaining and fun the year round.

State year $3.95

Llewellyn's DAILY PLANETARY GUIDE and ASTROLOGER'S DATE-BOOK: Includes all of the major daily aspects plus their exact times in Eastern and Pacific time zones, lunar phases, signs and voids plus their times, planetary motion, a monthly ephemeris, sunrise and sunset tables, special articles on the planets, signs, aspects, a business guide, planetary hours, rulerships, and much more. Large 5¼ X 8 format for more writing space, spiral bound to lay flat, address and phone listings, time zone conversion chart and blank horoscope chart.   **State year $6.95**

Llewellyn's ASTROLOGICAL CALENDAR: Large wall calendar of 52 pages. Beautiful full color cover and color inside. Includes special feature articles by famous astrologers, introductory information on astrology, Lunar Gardening Guide, celestial phenomena for the year, a blank horoscope chart for your own chart data, and monthly date pages which include aspects, lunar information, planetary motion, ephemeris, personal forecasts, lucky dates, planting and fishing dates, and more. 10 x 13 size. Set in Central time, with conversion table for other time zones worldwide.   **State year $6.95**

THE GODDESS BOOK OF DAYS
by Diane Stein

Diane Stein has created this wonderful guide to the Goddesses and festivals for every day of the year! This beautifully illustrated perpetual datebook will give you a listing for every day of the special Goddesses associated with that date along with plenty of room for writing in your appointments. It is a hardbound book for longevity, and has over 100 illustrations of Goddesses from around the world and from every culture. This is sure to have a special place on your desk. None other like it!

0-87542-758-8, 300 pgs., hardbound, 5¼ x 8, illus.   **$12.95**

WICCA: A Guide for the Solitary Practitioner
by Scott Cunningham

Wicca is a book of life, and how to live magically, spiritually, and wholly attuned with Nature. It is a book of sense and common sense, not only about Magick, but about religion and one of the most critical issues of today: how to achieve the much needed and wholesome relationship with our Earth. Cunningham presents Wicca as it is today—a gentle, Earth-oriented religion dedicated to the Goddess and God. This book fulfills a need for a practical guide to solitary Wicca—a need which no previous book has fulfilled.

Here is a positive, practical introduction to the religion of Wicca, designed so that any interested person can learn to practice the religion alone, anywhere in the world. It presents Wicca honestly and clearly, without the pseudo-history that permeates other books. It shows that Wicca is a vital, satisfying part of twentieth century life.

This book presents the theory and practice of Wicca from an individual's perspective. The section on the Standing Stones Book of Shadows contains solitary rituals for the Esbats and Sabbats. This book, based on the author's nearly two decades of Wiccan practice, presents an eclectic picture of various aspects of this religion. Exercises designed to develop magical proficiency, a self-dedication ritual, herb, crystal and rune magic, recipes for Sabbat feasts, are included in this excellent book.

ISBN:0-87542-118-0, 240 pgs., illus., 6 x 9 $9.95

THE CRONE'S BOOK OF WORDS
by Valerie Worth

The Crone's Book of Words contains rituals and spells to avert temptation, win another's love, recall one who is unfaithful, overcome insomnia, seek that which has been lost, atone for cutting down a tree, to train a familiar, to see the future, to keep hair from falling, for gathering herbs, to defeat tobacco, to bring rain, and much more. Magic *is* alive, and Magic is afoot in the world today in the words spoken, read, sung, or only imagined. Here is Magic to enjoy, and Magic to use: Magic to shape reality according to human will. Here is not the Magic of ceremony, of expensive robes and complex paraphernalia, nor of formulae calling for ingredients from the far ends of earth. This Magic is from the heart, this Magic sings in a woman's voice and is shaped with a woman's hands; it is the Magic incarnate in every woman for every woman knows of the Power within.

Valerie Worth—poet, wise woman, student of the occult—has created from her studies of Nature, Folklore and Magic these poems that are instructions, incantations and spells for nearly every purpose, from the personal to the universal. She bases her work on certain premises: that words themselves are a means to control exteior phenomena and interior changes; that magic today is the same craft that it has always been; and that all rituals spring from the same vision of life made meaningful.

0-87542-891-6, 160 pgs. 5¼ x 8 $6.95

**THE LLEWELLYN PRACTICAL GUIDE TO CREATIVE VISUALI-
ZATION.** All things you will ever want must have their start in your
mind. The average person uses very little of the full creative power that is
his, potentially. It's like the power locked in the atom—it's all there, but
you have to learn to release it and apply it constructively.

**IF YOU CAN SEE IT . . . in your Mind's Eye . . . you will have it!
It's true: you can have whatever you want—but there are "laws"
to Mental Creation that must be followed. The power of the mind
is not limited to, nor limited by, the Material World—Creative
Visualization enables Man to reach beyond, into the Invisible
World of Astral and Spiritual Forces.**

Some people apply this innate power without actually knowing what
they are doing, and achieve great success and happiness; most people,
however, use this same power, again unknowingly, INCORRECTLY,
and experience bad luck, failure, or at best unfulfilled life.
This book changes that. Through an easy series of step-by-step, pro-
gressive exercises, your mind is applied to bring desire into realization!
Wealth, Power, Success, Happiness . . . even Psychic Powers . . . even
what we call Magickal Power and Spiritual Attainment . . . all can be
yours. You can easily develop this completely natural power, and correc-
tly apply it, for your immediate and practical benefit. Illustrated with uni-
que, "puts-you-into-the-picture" visualization aids.

0-87542-183-0, 255 pages, 5¼ x 8, softcover. $7.95
SUPPLEMENTAL DEEP MIND TAPE

THE LLEWELLYN DEEP MIND TAPE FOR ASTRAL PROJECTION.
This is a tool so powerful that it is offered only for use in conjunction with
the above book. The authors of this book are adepts fully experienced in
all levels of psychic development and training, and have designed this
90-minute cassette tape to guide the student through full relaxation and
all the preparations for projection, and then—with the added dimension
of the authors personally produced electronic synthesizer patterns of
sound and music—they program the Deep Mind through the stages of
awakening, and projection of, the astral Body of Light. And then the
programming guides your safe return to normal consciousness with
memory—enabling you to bridge the worlds of Body, Mind and Spirit.

**The Deep Mind Tape is a powerful new technique combining
guided Mind Programming with specially created sound and
music to evoke deep level response in the psyche and its psychic
centres for controlled development, and induction of the OUT-
OF-BODY EXPERIENCE.**

0-87542-168-7, 90-minute cassette tape. $9.95

Note: If you have the book, THE LLEWELLYN PRACTICAL GUIDE TO ASTRAL PROJECTION, you may order
this DEEP MIND TAPE by sending full price, plus $1.50 postage & handling ($7.00 overseas airmail). Or,
you can order both Book AND Tape for a special price of just $15.00 Postpaid in U.S.A. ($25.00 overseas
airmail).

THE TRUTH ABOUT WITCHCRAFT TODAY
by Scott Cunningham

This is a book written for the non-practitioner. It is intended to inform the public about the true nature of Wicca and to explode the myths often associated with it.

Religion is perhaps the most personal sphere of our lives—Because of this, much confusion exists between members of different religions.

There are those who use religion to oppress others, to vanquish civil rights and to suppress freedom of thought. This is exactly what has occured to practitioners of Witchcraft in the last 500 years. The public image of Witchcraft is falsely confused with murder, orgies, drug use and something called "Satanism."

The truth about Witchcraft is far different. It is Wicca—a religion, and folk magic—a natural practice. Hundreds of thousands of rational, sane persons are worshipping Goddesses and Gods unknown to outsiders. Many thousands of people are discovering how to utilize natural energies to create specific, positive changes in their lives.

This book is a call for reason. It is an attempt to explode the myths about two practices which have been with us from the beginning of human thought. It is, indeed, *The Truth About Witchcraft Today.*

0-87542-127-X, 200 pgs., mass market format   **$3.95**

THE INNER WORLD OF FITNESS
Melita Denning

Because the artificialities and the daily hassles of routine living tend to turn our attention from the real values, *The Inner World of Fitness* leads us back by means of those natural factors in life which remain to us: air, water, sunlight, the food we eat, the world of nature, meditation, sexual love and the power of our own wishes—so that through these things we can re-link ourselves in awareness to the great non-material forces of life and of being which underlie them.

The unity and interaction of inner and outer, keeping body and psyche open to the great currents of life and of the natural forces, is seen as the essential secret of *youthfulness* and hence of radiant fitness. Regardless of our physical age, so long as we are within the flow of these great currents, we have the vital quality of youthfulness: but if we begin to close off or turn away from those contacts, in the same measure we begin to lose youthfulness.

0-87542-165-2, 240 pgs., 5¼ x 8, softcover.   **$7.95**